A
DISCOURSE
BY
THREE DRUNKARDS
ON
GOVERNMENT

NAKAE CHŌMIN

A
DISCOURSE
BY
THREE DRUNKARDS
ON
GOVERNMENT

BY
NAKAE CHŌMIN
TRANSLATED BY
NOBUKO TSUKUI

EDITED
AND WITH AN INTRODUCTION
BY NOBUKO TSUKUI AND
JEFFREY HAMMOND

BOSTON   WEATHERHILL   LONDON

Weatherhill
An imprint of Shambhala Publications, Inc.
Horticultural Hall
300 Massachusetts Avenue
Boston, Massachusetts 02115
www.shambhala.com

Publication of this book was assisted by a grant from the Japan Foundation.
UNESCO COLLECTION OF REPRESENTATIVE WORKS, Japanese Series.
This book has been accepted in the Japanese Series of the Translations
Collection of the United Nations Educational, Scientific, and Cultural
Organization (UNESCO).

Frontispiece photograph of Nakae Chōmin courtesy of Iwanami Shoten, Tokyo.
Jacket design incorporates a comic drawing from *Toba-e Ōgi no Mato*, a wood-
block-printed book of 1720.

First edition, 1984
Eighth printing, 2010

Printed in the United States of America

⊛ This edition is printed on acid-free paper that meets the American National
Standards Institute Z39.48 Standard.
♻ Shambhala Publications makes every effort to print on recycled paper.
For more information please visit www.shambhala.com.
Distributed in the United States by Random House, Inc.,
and in Canada by Random House of Canada Ltd

Library of Congress Cataloging in Publication Data: Nakae, Chōmin, 1847–1901./A
discourse by three drunkards on government./Translation of: San suijin keirin
mondō./1. Political science. I. Tsukui, Nobuko. II. Hammond, Jeffrey A. III.
Title./JA69. J3N31813 1984 320 84-3666/ISBN 978-0-8348-0192-9

CONTENTS

5

FOREWORD

When the *Discourse by Three Drunkards on Government* (*Sansuijin Keirin Mondō*) appeared in 1887, Meiji Japan was nearing a turning point. An authoritarian government was completing work on a constitution that had been promised for the end of the decade. This charter, the first of its kind to be drawn up outside the Western world, would bring to completion two decades of study and experimentation with governmental forms. Advocates of representative government, who styled themselves the Movement for Freedom and People's Rights, had called for a share in power since 1874. Their awareness had been quickened by a flood of treatises and translations that related representative institutions to national strength. Nakae Chōmin had played a major role in that movement through the vigor and the elegance of his renditions of eighteenth-century French political discourse, in which he blended Confucian terminology and values with the thought of Rousseau. Other writers and translators harked to English utilitarianism and the philosophy of Herbert Spencer to call for sweeping changes in Japanese culture and values to conform with the laws of social progress. Although it was clear that the constitution would be granted by the authorities and not wrested from them, Nakae and other intellectuals had spent almost a de-

7

cade discussing ways in which it might nevertheless be transformed to serve as a challenge and spur to freedom rather than remain a passive accommodation to authority.

The international environment posed equally challenging problems. Japan's relative position in the competitive world of power politics seemed to be deteriorating. France had recently dealt China a humiliating defeat. In Korea, Japanese liberal-movement activists' efforts to affect change had been so firmly repulsed by Korean conservatives that China had been the gainer, and the Japanese liberals, who included among their number some of Nakae's old friends in the study of French, were temporarily out of action. The Meiji government itself was trying to negotiate recovery of its sovereignty through abolition of the unequal treaties with which it had been saddled, but within months revelation of the compromises the government was prepared to make would rekindle political party agitation and bring Nakae back into the political arena.

The setting was thus tremulous with anticipation and apprehension. Nakae's treatise had considerable popularity when it appeared. It experienced a second and perhaps even greater surge of interest sixty years later, after Japan's defeat in World War II. It is not difficult to account for either period of interest. Nakae focused much of his discourse on the issues of pacifism and national defense, topics that were no less compelling in the second half of the twentieth century, after Japan's postwar course had been set by men who decided that national well-being was more important than national strength. Nakae would have agreed.

Nakae's career places the dilemmas of the Meiji intellectual into sharp focus. He knew, had profited from, and indeed was a product of the Meiji government's concern with the transmission of Western learning. He had been sent by the authorities of his native fief of Tosa to study English and French at Nagasaki in pre-Meiji years, and there he had formed an admiration for the hero of the Meiji Restoration, Sakamoto Ryōma. From Nagasaki he made his way to Yokohama, where he acted as translator for the French minister and came to know early Meiji pioneers of Western learning like Mitsukuri Rinshō, Ōi Kentarō, and Fukui Gen'ichiro. Sponsored by the government as a special student of French in Tokyo, he appealed personally to Ōkubo Toshimichi to be assigned as a government-funded student in France. He reached Lyon as a student attached to the Iwakura mission of 1871 and remained there until 1874. After his recall he continued in government employment, first as an educator and then as a secretary. While he organized his own academy for the study of French (1874–86), he continued to rely on government sponsorship for the translation and publication of numerous works on French law and institutions. The Meiji Constitution of 1889 provided Nakae with further possibilities for public service; he was elected from Osaka's Fourth District (with 1,352 of the 2,041 votes cast) in Japan's first national election. Professor Kuwabara notes that Nakae could describe Japan's goal as "the creation of a Europeanized nation in Asia" in language almost identical to that used by government leaders.[1] Yet there were also important differences between Nakae and the Meiji leaders. Nakae's values remained explicitly Confucian, he had grave doubts about the need for burdensome military spending, and he believed in the importance of fully representative government.

Consequently Nakae also had a deep suspicion and distrust of his government; he knew from his Western reading that freedoms granted from above were less secure than those won from below. It seemed to him that Japan's problem was to transform the government's gift into the people's achievement. His efforts in this regard, through translations and through essays, were frequently obstructed by the Meiji government. The *Oriental Liberty Newspaper*

(*Tōyō Jiyu Shimbun*), established in 1881 with Nakae as editor and the court noble Saionji Kimmochi as president, ceased publication when the throne ordered Saionji to resign. Nakae mocked this prohibition in sardonic terms as "heaven's will," and risked prosecution for even this oblique reference to the sovereign. Nakae's editorials for the Liberal Party newspaper also invited censorship, and later, in 1887, his criticism of the government's apparent leniency on treaty reform saw him banished from the environs of the capital city of Tokyo.

Nakae's ambivalence toward his government was very nearly matched by his disillusion with the leaders of the movement for representative government. He had contempt for what seemed to him the short-sighted willingness of Itagaki Taisuke and Gotō Shōjirō to compromise with the ruling oligarchy at key points in Meiji political history. When his efforts to organize party representatives in the first Diet to demand procedural and substantive changes in constitutional practice were unsuccessful, and when the Tosa men compromised with the government instead, he resigned his Diet seat only three months after assuming it, with the contemptuous explanation that he feared his alcoholism would hinder his performance.

Nakae's subsequent efforts to make his way in the private sector were unfailingly disastrous. A series of business ventures which ranged from railroads and lumbering in Hokkaido to publishing firms ended in failure. His self-deprecation extended to establishment of a brothel, which he defended as no less appropriate to ordinary Japanese than the more elegant, and less criticized, arrangements that were made for powerful officials on the geisha circuit.

Indifferent to the opinions of the establishment of his day, Nakae was nevertheless a genuinely patriotic Meiji man. He was concerned for Japan's future in a day when the nation was inundated with Western thought and theory, coerced by unequal treaties with the Western powers, and bordered by ineffective states on the Asian continent. His objections to unthinking acceptance of Western theory can be seen in the answers his *Discourse* makes to the Gentleman of Western Learning, whose utopian conception of international relations governed by a Panglossian view of evolutionary improvement bears so little relation to the world of the 1880s in which he lived. Nakae relented in his criticism of reformer Gotō Shojirō long enough to compose the manifesto of the league Gotō formed in 1887 denouncing the government's proposed compromises with the Western powers. In turn, Asia seemed for him an object lesson and at times an opportunity. Although he recognized the error and danger of liberal activists' efforts to sponsor change in Korea on their own, his friendship with Ōi Kentarō, who had been at the forefront of that movement, was among his warmest. The discourse of his Champion of the East, ultimately unsatisfactory and superficial, undoubtedly relates to that contact with Ōi and to Nakae's participation in the league formed by Konoe Atsumaro in 1900 to focus public attention on the dangers posed by Russian activity in northeast Asia. "If we defeat Russia," Nakae told Kōtoku Shūsui, "we expand to the continent and bring peace to Asia; if we lose, our people will awaken from their dream."

So complex, ironic, and often sardonic a figure is difficult to structure and to analyze. The inconclusive nature of Nakae's *Discourse* speaks revealingly of the conflicting tides of ideas in which Nakae's writings played so large a role. While an intimate of the great of Meiji society, he also sided with the outcastes of Osaka, the Ainu of Hokkaido, and, indeed, with subject peoples everywhere. Fully aware of the problems the Meiji constitutional structure might bring, he nevertheless hoped that patience and education could make it a vehicle for the "god of evolution" and the future of Japan. Resolutely opposed to slavish imitation of nine-

11

teenth-century Western intellectual fashions, he found more in common with the questioning of the eighteenth-century philosophers whose writings reinforced his own aversion to organized religion. In his last work, written while he lay dying of cancer of the throat, he credited the ultimate success of Japan's modernization to the Japanese people's practicality and freedom from religious dogma.[3]

Sixty years later, as defeat in the Pacific War produced the results that Nakae, in 1900, had predicted would follow from defeat by Russia, his *Discourse*'s discussion of utopian pacifism had new relevance to Japan's struggle to reconcile the prohibition on armaments of Article IX of the new constitution with the realities of the international environment. It is not difficult to imagine the ironic smile, or perhaps toast, with which Nakae might have responded to the assurance of Tosa's Yoshida Shigeru and his followers that, although the new constitution clearly outlawed war as an instrument of national policy, common sense nevertheless required some provision for national defense. Thus in some sense the argument between the Gentleman of Western Learning and the Champion of the East has been going on for almost a century. That is why Nakae so often seems to speak as a contemporary.

MARIUS B. JANSEN
Princeton University

[1] Kuwabara Takeo, *Japan and Western Civilization* (Tokyo: University of Tokyo Press, 1983), p. 144.
[2] Quoted by Kōno Kenji, *Nakae Chōmin* (*Chūō Kōron, Nihon no Meichō*, vol. 36, Tokyo, 1970), p. 36. See also the dissertation by Margarat B. Dardess, "The Thought and Politics of Nakae Chōmin (1847–1901)" (Columbia University, 1973), which in-

cludes an appendix translation of the *Discourse* that was also issued as Occasional Paper No. 10 of the Western Washington State College in 1977, for further discussion of Nakae's views of China.

[3] Kuwabara, *op. cit.*, p. 80.

PREFACE

As a Japanese who has lived for an equal number of years in Japan and in the United States, I have been increasingly intested in the cross-cultural studies produced over the past two decades. Although my undergraduate and graduate majors were in American and British literature, my subsequent teaching and research have led me further into studying the relations and interactions of Occidental and Oriental cultures. My examination of the American poet Ezra Pound's work on the Japanese Noh drama, published in 1983 as *Ezra Pound and Japanese Noh Plays*, is one product of this pursuit. The completion of the present translation of Nakae Chōmin's work marks a deeply rewarding culmination of my professional and scholarly examination of two very different cultures.

When *Sansuijin Keirin Mondō* (A Discourse by Three Drunkards on Government) first came to my attention as a possible translation project, my knowledge of its author Nakae Chōmin was very limited. Moreover, the general characterization of this work as a classic statement of the political philosophy of the Meiji era made me hesitate to undertake its translation because my specialization is in neither Japanese history nor political science. At the same time, however, my curiosity about the book and its intriguing title was aroused. Reading Chōmin's book in the original was an unforgettable experience. I discovered a unique, powerful, intellectually stimulating work written by a philosopher turned political activist who had a strong sense of his mission as a purveyor of solutions to the problems faced by Japan of the Meiji era. I found myself fascinated with the book in every respect: its dramatic setting with three masterfully drawn characters; its gripping, dynamic style of writing; its penetrating insight into the political, philosophical, and historical characteristics of various nations of Europe, Asia, and America; and, above all, its timelessness. The *Discourse* deals with the future course of Japan and its options for survival. These most fundamental problems that faced Japan of the 1880s are still very much in evidence today. By the time I finished reading the book, I knew I wanted to translate it, not as a text meant exclusively for students and specialists in Japanese history or political science but as an extraordinary work to be enjoyed and appreciated by a wider audience in the English-speaking world.

Although an earlier, abridged English translation of this work exists in the form of an occasional paper, the present volume offers a complete and authentic version of the Japanese text; the translation presented here reflects the book's stature not only as a historical document or a treatise on political philosophy but as a literary masterpiece as well. I am convinced that this work will have a wide appeal to Western readers, who will discover that its author was very much at home with European culture—not only its history, philosophy, politics, and economics, but also its customs and manners, even to the point of having his characters enjoy a particular brand of cognac well known in Europe at the time. Chōmin's familiarity with Western culture is especially impressive because he wrote the book

in the early years of the Meiji era (1868–1912), which followed the long period of Japan's feudal isolation.

My main concern as a translator has been to successfully
convey the force, the charm, and the verve of the original.
The translation from the Japanese into English is entirely
my work, and I am solely responsible for its accuracy. I
am also solely responsible for the factual verity of the introduction. In an effort to enhance the literary qualities of
the English version, I was fortunate enough to have my col-
league, Professor Jeffrey Hammond, collaborate with me
in editing the translation. Though Professor Hammond does
not read Japanese, he possesses a keen sensitivity to language and experience in the art of translation. In addition,
his knowledge of Western culture and literature and his
critical and insightful reading of Chōmin's *Discourse* con-
tributed significantly to the writing of the introduction.
In the last stage of editing and polishing the text and the
introduction, Professor Hammond and I worked together to
present the best possible English version. Throughout the
translation we have tried to adhere to the original as much
as possible in the letter as well as the spirit, in form as well
as substance. The only significant departure from this principle is paragraphing. The present version has a greater
number of paragraphs than the original Japanese text as a
means of achieving greater clarity and ease of comprehen-
sion.

I am immensely gratified that this translation has the
honor of being included in the UNESCO Collection of
Representative Works—an indication of the growing interest in Chōmin and his writings. This interest is reflected
as well in the recent growth of scholarship and criticism
dealing with Chōmin. The translation and the introduction
in the present volume have benefited from this growth,
especially the work on Chōmin produced in the past two

17

decades. Two works stand out as most important: the authoritative original text of *Sansuijin Keirin Mondō,* edited by professors Kuwabara Takeo and Shimada Kenji, which contains a modern Japanese translation, notes, and commentary; and *Nakae Chōmin no Sekai* (The World of Nakae Chōmin), edited by Kinoshita Junji and Etō Fumio, which is a compilation of papers presented at the 1975 seminar on *Sansuijin Keirin Mondō* held in Tokyo as well as additional original articles. (More detailed information on these and other scholarly publications can be found in the "Notes to the Introduction.")

I would like to thank Clint Newman, who first suggested the translation of this work and continued to give his support and encouragement throughout the project. I also appreciate the generous help and advice of Professor Takeo Kuwabara in many ways, both during the preparation of the manuscript and afterward.

For their encouragement and help at various stages of the project, I wish to express my gratitude to professors Tetsuo Najita, Earl Miner, Paul A. Olson, Marius Jansen, Ineko Kondo, Tetsuya Kataoka, Eizaburō Okuizumi, and Dr. Ronald Morse; to Mr. Thaddeus Ōta and Ms. Fumi Norcia of the Library of Congress; to Mr. Kikuo Itaya and Mr. Sakuo Hotta of Tokyo; to my sister Reiko Numao and brother Tomizō Tsukui; and not the least of all to my editor, Mr. Jeffrey Hunter of John Weatherhill, Inc.

I complete this step in research on Chōmin's life and his works with great admiration for his idealism, his courage, his integrity, and, above all, his pround concern for the human condition. It will be most gratifying to me if the present volume contributes to a greater understanding of Chōmin, an extraordinary man and thinker who has yet not received the recognition he deserves.

NOBUKO TSUKUI

18

INTRODUCTION

THE SIGNIFICANCE OF NAKAE CHŌMIN'S LIFE is reflected in his selection of his pen name; Chōmin literally means "a billion or trillion people."[1] A strong advocate of popular rights, democracy, and equality in late nineteenth-century Japan, Chōmin "never for a moment doubted that the people were sovereign."[2] In addition, as a pioneer of French studies in Japan, he was widely known as the "Rousseau of the Orient." Some two thousand disciples studied at his French academy, and Chōmin exerted a tremendous influence on the dissemination of European political theory in Japan.

Born Nakae Tokusuke on November 1, 1847, in Kōchi, of the *han*, or feudal domain, of Tosa, Chōmin was a quiet, bookish child.[3] His father was a low-ranking samurai stationed mostly in Edo, and Chōmin, the first son, was brought up chiefly by his mother. When his father died in 1861, Chōmin became the head of the household, inheriting his father's samurai rank of *ashigaru*, the lowest rank of foot soldier. In April of the following year, when the Bunbukan, the *han* school, was opened, Chōmin was immediately enrolled to study Chinese, English, and Dutch. In 1865, he was sent to Nagasaki as one of the official *han* students, where he studied French. Two years later, Chōmin left for Edo to continue his French studies at Murakami Eishun's academy. Although he was soon expelled for his frequent visits to houses of prostitution, Chōmin continued to study French under a Catholic priest in Yokohama. In December, on the occasion of the opening of Hyōgo Harbor and the Osaka market, Chōmin went to Hyōgo as interpreter for the French diplomatic delegation.

In 1868, the year of the Meiji Restoration, Chōmin became acquainted with such future political leaders as Mutsu Munemitsu and Nakajima Nobuyuki. In May of the following year, Chōmin entered an academy in Tokyo run by Mitsukuni Rinshō, scholar of law as well as French and Dutch. At about the same time Chōmin began to study the Buddhist canon. He also taught French at two academies, one of which later became Tokyo Imperial University. In 1871, with the help of Ōkubo Toshimichi, Chōmin was selected to go to France as a low-level appointee in the Ministry of Justice. In November, Chōmin and the other selected students left Yokohama for Europe, by way of the United States, together with the delegation led by Ambassador Plenipotentiary Iwakura Tomomi. From October 1872 to May 1874, when all government students abroad were ordered to return to Japan, Chōmin lived in Lyon and later in Paris. During his stay, Chōmin's Japanese associates included future leaders Saionji Kimmochi and Kōmyōji Saburō. He also studied under Émile Acollas, the progressive political philosopher. In June 1874, a summary of Chōmin's account of the French election was published in *Shimbun Zasshi* (Newspaper Journal).

After his return to Japan, Chōmin started an academy for French studies in his own home in Tokyo. In February 1875, he was appointed President of Tokyo Gaikokugo Gakkō (Tokyo Foreign Languages Institute), but resigned after serving less than three months. Shortly afterward, he took a job as a clerk for the Genrōin, a non-elective body

20

created to discuss legislative matters. He kept this job for two years; after that, he never again worked for the government as a civil servant. In the meantime, Chomin continued to run his French academy.

The beginning of Japan's popular-rights movement coincided with Chōmin's return from France in 1874, when Itagaki Taisuke and others presented a petition for establishing an elected parliament. Although Chōmin did not join the movement immediately, he tried to provide theoretical support by introducing democratic ideas through French studies, an effort reflected in part by his translation, issued in 1882, of Rousseau's *Contrat Social*. Chōmin also helped start *Tōyō Jiyū Shimbun* (Oriental Liberty Newspaper), with Saionji Kimmochi as its president and Chōmin as editor-in-chief. Beginning publication on March 18, 1881, this was the first Japanese newspaper to use the word *jiyū* (liberty) in the title. The government, attempting to suppress demands for popular rights, forced Saionji to resign, and the paper ceased publication after only thirty-four issues.

Despite such attempts at suppression, the rapid increase in support for popular rights prompted Iwakura Tomomi to remark that "the state of things on the eve of the French Revolution must not have been greatly different from what we have here now."[4] However, disunity among the anti-government forces weakened efforts at reform. Some radical members of the Jiyūtō party even resorted to violence, resulting in the anti-government riots known as the Gumma and Kabasan Incidents. Frightened by these disturbances, the more moderate Jiyūtō leaders dissolved the party in October 1884.

In the midst of this turmoil, Chōmin took very little direct political action. Strongly opposed to violence, he devoted himself to refining his political theories. In the process, he translated Veron's *L'Esthétique* in 1883 and

21

Fouillée's *Histoire de la Philosophie* in 1886, both published by the Ministry of Education. He also wrote, in 1886, *Rigaku Kōgen* (Introduction to Philosophy) and *Kakumeizen Furansu Niseiki no Koto* (France During the Two Centuries Before the Revolution). Written one year later, Chōmin's *Sansuijin Keirin Mondō* (A Discourse by Three Drunkards on Government) represents another—and perhaps his most celebrated—attempt at working out his political philosophy.

However, Chōmin found that he could not remain content as a scholar dedicated only to political theory in the abstract. Shortly after the *Discourse* appeared, the opposition to proposed revisions in Japan's treaties with Western nations rekindled a widespread movement led by a coalition of popular rights groups to overthrow the existing regime. Chōmin became an active participant, and played a central role by composing an influential indictment of the government.

These new developments prompted the government to issue the infamous security ordinance of 1887, and Chōmin was one of 570 political activists, including Ozaki Yukio, who were expelled from Tokyo. On December 30, Chōmin boarded a train for Osaka. During his forced exile, Chōmin started the *Shinonome Shimbun* (Newspaper of the Dawn), dedicated to spreading the idea of popular rights in anticipation of the establishment of Parliament. The central mission of the paper was to provide a basis for examining the constitution that was about to be granted by the emperor, so that it might be made as democratic as possible. In addition, Chōmin called for complete emancipation of the *burakumin*, or members of Japan's lowest caste, in his February 1888 editorial entitled "Shimmin Sekai" (The World of New Citizens). With the establishment of the constitution on February 11, 1889, the order of expulsion was officially rescinded, and Chōmin and his family returned to Tokyo in October.

22

Some months prior to this, a movement to elect Chōmin to Japan's first Parliament had begun, and supporters decided to send him to the Lower House. Running from the fourth district in Osaka, he was elected in the July 1 parliamentary election. Meanwhile, Chōmin continued his journalistic activities. In the fall the Rikken Jiyūtō (Constitutional Liberty Party) was established, and in January 1891, the new party's official newspaper, *Rikken Jiyū Shimbun* (Constitutional Liberty Newspaper), began publication with Chōmin as editor-in-chief. On February 4, the paper was ordered to suspend publication for fifteen days. When publication resumed, Chōmin attacked the timidity of the Lower House in a scathing editorial entitled "Muketsuchu no Chinretsujo" (The Exhibition Hall of Bloodless Bugs). On the same day he submitted his resignation from the Lower House. On February 27, representatives of the voters from Chōmin's district asked him to reconsider, but on March 1, the Lower House voted ninety-four to ninety-three to accept his resignation.

After four months of extensive travel in Hokkaido, Chōmin returned to Tokyo to care for his ailing mother, who died shortly thereafter. During the next eight years, he tried various business ventures to help finance his political activities and his writing. In order to save money, he even gave up the drinking for which he had long been well known. But despite his determination, he failed in virtually every business he tried, and was finally reduced to poverty.

Even during this period, however, his literary activity did not cease. He translated Schopenhauer's *Grundprobleme der Ethik* from a French version, and in December 1897 he almost single-handedly formed the Kokumintō (People's Party) and became the editor of its official monthly publication. The Kokumintō party called for universal suffrage, tuition-free elementary education, and freedom of speech and publishing.

23

In the spring of 1901, during a business trip to Osaka, Chōmin learned that he was suffering from cancer and that he had only a year and a half to live. During his final months, he struggled to complete his last two books, *Ichinen Yūhan* (A Year and a Half) and *Zoku Ichinen Yūhan* (Continuation of A Year and a Half). He died at home in Tokyo on December 13, 1901, at the age of fifty-four. In accordance with his will, no religious rite was performed, but a memorial service was attended by many mourners, including his disciples and such well-known political figures as Itagaki Taisuke and Ōishi Masami, who delivered memorial addresses.

Sansuijin Keirin Mondō (A Discourse by Three Drunkards on Government), one of Chōmin's most important works, was published as a single volume in May 1887. The first part of the book had appeared a month earlier in a magazine, *Kokumin no Tomo* (People's Companion), under the title, "Suijin no Kiron" (Strange Ideas of a Drunkard). The value and influence of the *Discourse* were felt almost immediately. Kōtoku Shūsui, Chōmin's most important disciple, lists the book as one of the chief sources for his socialist ideas.[5] More recently, Professor Kuwabara Takeo has called the *Discourse* a representative classic of the Meiji era (1868–1912) which can still be read with a sense of urgency, and the most outstanding literary piece of the period in the depth of its ideas.[6]

The *Discourse* was written at a crucial time in Chōmin's life.[7] Before writing this book, Chōmin had devoted himself to providing theoretical support to the popular rights movement, but the writing of the *Discourse* marked the beginning of Chōmin's active involvement with practical politics. Chōmin clearly conceived of the *Discourse* as a major statement and poured all his experience of forty years and all his learning in political philosophy into its composition.[8] Further, the *Discourse* marks a turning point in Japanese political history. Written at a time when popular rights

24

movements were under attack, the work suggests directions in which the reform movement might be reconstructed.[9] As Professor Tetsuo Najita puts it, Chōmin "allowed himself to argue . . . the possibility of the steady expansion of human freedom in modern Japan through intellectual dispute and political struggle, even though objective conditions, including the constitutional order, might turn out to be far less than ideal."[10] At its most basic level, the work reflects Chōmin's attempt to merge political idealism with practical politics.

And yet the *Discourse* does not deal with the Japanese political scene in a direct way; the book makes no mention, for example, of the current deterioration of the popular rights movement. Instead, the focus is on international relations.[11] Evidently, Chōmin's purpose was not so much to discuss specific domestic issues as to acquaint his readers with the Western concept of democracy that was fundamental to the movement and to the constitutional government that was about to come into being. Through the words of three characters—a host and two guests—Chōmin discusses the concept of democracy and the future of the nation. What course should Japan take as a small, less "civilized" country faced with imminent threats to its independence? How can the nation assume a role as a pioneer of Asian nationalism without becoming a follower of European imperialism? These are the major issues debated by the host, Master Nankai (Nankai Sensei), and the guests, the Gentleman of Western Learning (Yōgaku Shinshi), and the Champion of the East (Gōketsu no Kyaku). Significantly, these are also questions central to Chōmin's entire political and philosophical career.[12]

The *Discourse* is not, however, merely a vehicle through which Japan's options in foreign policy are explored. Although the work certainly provides an index of important political and social issues of the time, Chōmin managed to

25

invest the *Discourse* with substantial literary qualities as well. Like most classics, the *Discourse* at once fulfilled and surpassed the expectations of its readers. The debate genre, for example, had been prominent in Japanese literature for centuries.[13] Stemming from ancient Buddhist dialogues between master and disciple and reinforced by the introduction of the Christian catechism by Jesuit missionaries, the tradition of the philosophical debate as Chōmin received it was essentially a means by which opposing viewpoints could be set forth and argued. Like the characters in a Socratic dialogue, participants would find their misconceptions corrected and their thinking rectified by a tolerant Master who steered them toward an explicit conclusion. The discussion almost invariably left the reader with an unambiguous message.

But Chōmin alters this tradition in significant ways. For one thing, he does not depict Master Nankai as a controlling force who leads the speakers toward a "right" answer. To be sure, Master helps shape the overall structure of the debate by providing transitions from one speaker to the other and summarizing their views at the end, but he remains passive and detached throughout most of the discussion. Unlike other masters in Japanese literature, he refuses to impose an inductive path toward one truth or one revelation. As Maruyama Masao has pointed out, the *Discourse* does not preach a specific, absolute doctrine; rather, it presents several viewpoints without judging their relative worth.[14] It does not propose solutions as much as it explores the fallible but necessary process of finding solutions. Nor are Gentleman and Champion mere spokesmen for distinct ideological positions; they present multiple and partially overlapping viewpoints. Unlike many characters in Japanese debate literature, they are not easily reduced to one-dimensional advocates of clearly definable ideologies. Finally, the work is not constructed according to the

question-and-answer format of the traditional debate. Instead, the characters express their views through extended
monologues of various lengths. Gentleman, as the philoso-
pher-idealist, is much more talkative than the militaristic
Champion. His speech is nearly twice as long as Champion's. Champion's, on the other hand, is nearly twice
as long as Master's, who presents himself primarily as an on-
looker. Exchanges do occur, of course, but they generally
take the form of playful interruptions that serve to sharpen
the characterization or add dramatic interest.[15]

Chōmin's characters, perhaps more than any other element of the work, serve as a warning against viewing the
Discourse as a vehicle for expressing a dogmatic political
position. The rich characterization rescues the discussion
from the limitations of political allegory or thinly-veiled
propaganda. The effectiveness of the work results in part
from the emergence of the speakers as distinct human
beings, subject to the contradictions and faulty reasoning of
real people. Their rich ambiguity stems primarily from their
relationships to Chōmin himself. Despite their differences,
Gentleman, Champion, and Master all embody apparently
contradictory characteristics of the author and his political
philosophy.[16]

Gentleman, steeped in European learning and committed
to the idealisms of nineteenth-century European politics
and philosophy, clearly reflects Chōmin's extensive expo-
sure to and interest in Western thought, particularly the
political legacy of the French Revolution. Gentleman also,
of course, represents Chōmin as political activist as well
as philosopher. As the "Rousseau of the Orient," Chōmin
remained committed in his roles as translator, editor, and,
briefly, as elected representative, to the basic assumption
that government derives its right to govern from the people.
Indeed, his entire career could be viewed as an attempt to
introduce such European-inspired reforms in Japan. Chōmin

27

would certainly be highly sympathetic toward Gentleman's demands for democracy and peace. As one critic has pointed out, Gentleman presents a view of political reality as it *ought* to be.[17] It is Gentleman who defines Japan's future as a "child prodigy," as a potential showplace of justice and equality that would serve as a model for other nations. A true visionary, he looks to the future as the inevitable fulfillment of history's march toward democracy. For Gentleman, the future will be better; the primary issue is whether political leaders will quicken or retard the progressive betterment of mankind.

But Chōmin had no illusions about the extent to which such ideals could be put into practice in the Japan of his day. The limitations of wholesale and immediate implementation of European innovations are devastatingly satirized in the figure of Gentleman. Gentleman has, of course, a Western appearance, and his persistent appeal to the authority of "modern European scholars" lays him open to the charge of being a shallow follower of fashionable trends. He is, as Champion states, a true lover of novelty. Moreover, Gentleman's ideas, admirable as they seem, are presented in a way that exposes the impractical nature of his idealism. When asked, for example, what could be done in the event of an actual invasion of Japan, Gentleman naively denies the possibility of such an event. And when pressed for a solution, he admits that there is nothing much to do except to be shot.

Master and Champion both agree that Gentleman's ideas are scholarly but impractical, and the contradictions in his viewpoint make it clear that Chōmin does not intend for Gentleman to stand as an unassailable spokesman for pacifism. Gentleman bases much of his argument, for example, on his belief in the progressive thrust of history, that political systems will naturally and inevitably evolve toward pure democracy. We must, he asserts, join with and aid

View of Gentleman

in the progress of the god of evolution, if only to avoid becoming hopelessly mired in the restrictive confines of the past. Yet Gentleman chooses to ignore the other, darker side of the evolutionary model: that political evolution can be seen as the ongoing process of the strong overtaking the weak. In addition, Gentleman falls into the trap of imposing a clear and linear progression onto historical events (a trap that Master goes to some lengths to expose) and thus he commits the theorist's error of making fact subservient to theory and ideology. There is also a hint of danger in his ideas. At one point, for instance, he insists that equality and freedom be extended to all citizens, except, of course, those who are "retarded, insane, or otherwise troublesome in their behavior" or who "corrupt public morals or incite riots." Perhaps Chōmin's most telling attack on pure ideologues is the fact that Gentleman fails to say who would single out such citizens.[18] Finally, many of Gentleman's ideas are satirized by means of the very forcefulness of his statements, as when he imagines the possibility that Louis XVI could have graciously abdicated his powers and retired to the benign role of gentleman patriot. No Japanese reader familiar with the events leading up to the French Revolution could fail to see the irony of such an extremely idealistic image.

Champion

Champion provides a sharp contrast, and reflects Chōmin as a practical strategist. Champion describes what is, rather than what should be. As a nationalist, Chōmin was concerned with what he saw as Japan's weak and conciliatory policies toward Europe and the United States. Like Champion, he shared in the widespread fear that the traditional culture was on the verge of annihilation at the hands of the West and of young Japanese activists.[19] It would be wrong, of course, to find in this a basic inconsistency in Chōmin's thought. After all, Champion does not speak against democracy per se. Instead, he concerns himself primarily with external affairs, especially Japan's relationship to the Western powers. Chōmin himself at one point advocated an invasion of the Asian mainland, and his writings are permeated with the idea that if Japan is to enjoy social and political progress, it must first ensure its continued existence as an independent nation with its own culture and values.[20] Champion's somewhat flippant tone suggests the cynicism of a man who is quite aware of what it would mean to lose one's national identity. Champion is, according to his own distinctions, "nostalgic" for the elements of the traditional culture. Unlike Gentleman, he finds answers in the past, and perhaps because of this, prides himself on an ability to interpret history more objectively than Gentleman can. He also seems more aware of practical situations and realpolitik. Although he insists, for example, that his plans for invasion are suitable for the present time and place, he does not suggest that such a course would work for a European nation, or that it would by extension be useful in all eras and situations.

Chiefly because of his highly developed practicality, Champion is shrewder than Gentleman. For one thing, he seems to be the closer observer of human nature, as evidenced by his distinctions between the lovers of nostalgia and the lovers of novelty, the old and the young, and the rural and the urban. Moreover, he assesses himself accurately as a nostalgic lover of war—someone who misses the tradition and identity associated with the sword in medieval Japan. But his pragmatic view of history gives him a detachment that makes him capable of humor, usually at Gentleman's expense. Cheerfully agreeing, for example, that he and the nostalgia lovers constitute a cancer on society, he playfully tells Gentleman that such a cancer should simply be cut out of the body politic. Champion's comments here are certainly an ironic statement of a professional soldier's willingness to be sacrificed. Yet a further

30

irony is that what seems to be noble self-sacrifice turns out to be a backhanded quest for self-fulfillment. One way to cut out the cancer, of course, is to kill the lovers of nostalgia. Champion knows, however, that Gentleman's liberal ideology would never permit him to agree to this. The only remaining option, then, is to permit all the lovers of nostalgia to invade that "certain large nation" in Africa or Asia—a thinly veiled reference to China, of course—thus fulfilling Champion's goals. There, Champion half-jokingly asserts, he would set up a "cancer society" where he and his companions could presumably maintain military strength to their hearts' content. The small, original homeland would be left to the rest of the citizens—including Gentleman—to cultivate as a garden of liberty if they so desired. This illustration points up a significant contrast between the two debaters: while Gentleman occasionally falls into unintended and self-ridiculing irony, Champion can deliberately use irony as a devastating tool of debate.

But Champion is not without his own biases and misconceptions. Chōmin's commitment to reform would not permit him to allow Champion's reactionary statements to remain unqualified. As a man of action, Champion illustrates the dangers of rash action and cynicism. Unlike Gentleman, who suffers from a surfeit of vision, Champion suffers from a lack of it. His practicality fails precisely because it never transcends the restrictions of historical precedent. His view of history is nearsighted; although he sees the trees very clearly, he loses sight of the fact that people have the potential to change the forest. He thus finds a chilling inevitability in war, and takes no pains to conceal how much he relishes the fact. Champion's apparent detachment seems all the more disturbing because in his world—and ours—history seems to be on his side. Champion is also guilty of bolstering his arguments with absurd or simplistic analogies, such as his statement that the "stupidest" ani-

31

mals are those least capable of defense. His greatest weakness, however, arises from the fact that he operates from a romanticized view of war that is every bit as myopic, if not more so, than any of Gentleman's idealistic doctrines. Here, at least, is one instance in which Champion's irony is decidedly unintentional. When he describes the joys of planning a battle and dismisses the pain of wounded soldiers as inconsequential, he, too, emerges as a man who fails to root his ideas in reality. At this point, his love of battle is revealed as something quite idealistic; although he claims to relish the smell of gunpowder, the abstract tactics of battle are what he actually finds attractive.

Presiding over all of this, though mostly in the background, is the figure of Master Nankai, who repudiates both viewpoints. Characterizing Gentleman's views as "strong liquor" and Champion's as "harsh poison," Master reflects Chōmin as a practical idealist, interested in steering a middle course in social and political reform, seeking a balance between theory and application, reforming Japan without sacrificing her identity, and adapting lofty principles to the exigencies of practical politics. As one would expect in the debate tradition, Master maintains a tranquil detachment throughout most of the debate, sipping his drink and gently encouraging the others to clarify and elaborate their views. In so doing, of course, he permits them to undermine their own efforts, and his relative silence until the last section of the book suggests his amused disapproval of their ideas.[21]

His self-effacing, gentle manner in the earlier portions of the *Discourse* suggests the traditional figure of the enlightened philosopher who patiently hears out his pupils in order to correct their faults. But even from the very beginning, we see that this Master is not exactly the stock figure of Japanese debate literature. As we first meet him he is drinking happily, his thoughts roaming the entire span

32

of space and time. We are told that his geography and history do not always coincide with those of the real world—a fact that certainly liberates his thinking, but which might also serve to cast a faint shadow over whatever truths he might discover. Far from being an ascetic figure who eschews the pleasures of the world, Master enjoys his guests, the give-and-take of political debate, and, of course, his drink. Chōmin shrouds him with a quaint ambiguity; indeed, we find out at the end of the *Discourse* that Master's sense of time may be as detached from reality as are his history and geography. 阮希智服家

In reaction against the extreme views of the two visitors, Master's analysis of what Gentleman and Champion have said is astute and insightful. Characterizing their arguments as "empty words," he centers on the impracticality of Gentleman's views and the danger of Champion's. Clearly, neither offers a viable option for Japan's foreign policy. Extreme solutions might, in Chōmin's view, be amusing to pursue in the abstract context of debate, but through Master he reveals his impatience with such answers when real solutions for real problems must be found. Master attacks Champion, for instance, because Champion's policies would only alienate the Western powers that threaten Japan's integrity. Moreover, Master's objection to Champion's plan is at least partly practical in nature: China would simply be too strong to conquer. He attacks Gentleman at greater length, perhaps because of Chōmin's growing disenchantment with reformers who desired more changes than Japanese society could then accommodate. It may be, too, that the denigration of Gentleman reflects Chōmin's parodic treatment of his own reputation as a philosopher. 顶浪

Through his repudiation of both extremes, Master elucidates several simple truths. First, no one can presume to say with certainty exactly what historical events mean; to impose an ideological order on history is to undermine

33

the chances of real progress. Second, the nature of citizens'
rights is certainly determined in part by the means by
which they were obtained—that is, by the political system
in which they exist. But when Master insists that there is
no essential difference between the effects of retrieved and
bestowed rights, he reflects Chōmin's conviction that the
chief end of political progress—the securing of citizens'
rights—is more important than the means. Finally, and
perhaps most importantly, Chōmin's pragmatism is evident
in Master's insistence that social and political progress must
be gradual, and must never outstrip the capacity of a society
to absorb it. No doubt such a pragmatic view was fostered
in part by the censorship prevalent in Chōmin's era. His
rejection of extreme solutions most likely reflects his recognition that radical change was impossible under the
existing government. Chōmin's abiding pragmatism may
have been in part the product of a frustrated idealism, but
whatever its origin, his insistence upon practical solutions
was well suited to the task of pushing for reforms within
the limitations imposed by censorship and an oppressive
government.

Despite the semicomic figure Master presents at the
opening of the *Discourse*, insights such as these enable him
to assume some of the functions of the traditional teachers
found in debate literature. Like them, he exposes the fallacies of his pupils' arguments. Like them, he facilitates the
discussion and provides an atmosphere of tolerant exchange.
Unlike them, however, he keeps pouring the drinks. At one
point, he interrupts the debate in order to smile and observe
how much he's enjoying himself. The drinking prepares us
to face the fact that Master's position, when he finally gets
around to stating it, offers scarcely more real edification
than those of his guests. His plans for maintaining peace,
for example, are simplistic to say the least, and his assertion
that large arms buildups constitute little real danger pre-

34

cisely because they are so large is based on a concept of balance of power that seems at least as dangerous and naive as anything Champion and Gentleman have said. In addition, when Master addresses the same question that had been asked of Gentleman—how should the nation respond to an invasion?—his affirmation that "we must simply resist with all our strength" is followed by vague suggestions for defense and a seemingly naive hope that "our military people would naturally devise excellent strategies to deal with the invasion." In fact, the strategies Master briefly outlines suggest the guerrilla tactics that would one day prove so successful in Vietnam. But when it comes time for Master to reveal his domestic plans for Japan, his brief remarks advocating the adoption of European Constitutionalism are noticeably lacking in specifics: practical matters would take care of themselves, and rights would simply be bestowed gradually, as the people became ready to accept them. Even Champion and Gentleman are underwhelmed by Master's speech. Both agree that Master's ideas seem commonplace and self-evident, an anticlimactic conclusion to an extensive and important discussion.

In one sense, of course, Gentleman and Champion are correct. Readers expecting a political and philosophical tour de force from Master would be misreading the *Discourse* as a standard exercise in the debate genre. But there are, Chōmin seems to suggest, no simple answers. Or perhaps more accurately, simple answers are the only potentially workable answers. Gentleman and Champion present proposals that are as impractical as they are dazzling in their novelty. But such responses to Japan's political future were for Chōmin an irresponsible game, and represented in their own way another manifestation of the pervasive love of novelty that he ridicules. Through Master, Chōmin insists that determining Japan's foreign policy is not a mere contest in which different sides vie for dominance. Perhaps even more importantly, Master's simple solutions present a kind of vacuum at the end of the work, a void that readers are implicitly invited to fill with answers of their own. In this way, Chōmin offers the *Discourse* as a means to open up active discussion rather than as a final word that could serve only to close it.

Although Chōmin's masterpiece becomes in this sense a lesson that steadfastly refuses to be a lesson, the *Discourse* should by no means be seen as a reflection of the author's indifference. To be sure, Master at one point chides his hearers for worrying too much about wars and rumors of wars. Chōmin provides, however, a marginal gloss to the passage: "Master Nankai prevaricates." The problems addressed in the debate were uppermost in Chōmin's mind, and although he managed to retain a center of tranquility amid the "neurosis" of political concern, he had genuine fears that Japan would be swept up in a global conflict originating from Europe. One can also detect a sense of weary resignation in Master's remarks, which may well reflect Chōmin's recognition of himself as a man of ideas forced by the issues of the day to choose among several distasteful or hazardous courses of action.[22] When Master impatiently waves away any further explanation of his views, suggesting instead that the details of government could merely be worked out along the lines of the European model, he has been forced out of the Utopia of discussion, a Utopia where his mind can freely roam the universe, into a harsh world where real geography and history matter a great deal.[23]

Despite the seriousness of such a theme, however, the *Discourse* is pervaded with irony and lightened with flashes of subtle humor. The irony seems especially appropriate, perhaps even inevitable, in such a paradoxical book, a political work that avoids propaganda, written by a philosopher concerned with how to implement real social and political reform in a nation both attracted to and repelled by Western traditions.[24] The anticlimactic conclusion, the unresolved contradictions, the often ironic marginal glosses, the occasionally absurd analogies employed by all three speakers, the guiding presence of a Master who is reluctant to guide, the constant drinking—all these elements combine to produce a work very different from the usual political manifesto. The very title reminds us that we find definitive answers in this book only at the risk of being led by "three drunkards."

Chōmin's ability to resist casting his thoughts in dogmatic from and his refusal to insist on sweeping solutions to complex political issues helped elevate the *Discourse* into a classic of late nineteenth-century Japanese thought. The popularity of the work was aided by Chōmin's prose, a complex and highly figurative medium that can be only very roughly approximated in English. Perhaps least subject to loss in the process of translation are the exemplary vignettes used by all three speakers. Champion, for example, deftly distinguishes the older from the younger generation by showing how a man would respond to his child's use of a parasol or his wife's participation in political debate. Gentleman constructs elaborate analogies that compare democracy to summer and ideas to the yeast that produces fine beer. Master compares a military buildup to children rolling larger and larger snowballs. These vignettes illustrate the speakers' use of metaphor as argument. The parabolic style gives the entire work a charm that would be greatly diminished without it. At times, the vignettes are expanded into lyric passages of exquisite beauty, as in Gentleman's elaborate and impassioned hymn to democracy, or Master's beautiful comparison of social progress with the painting of a fine picture. Equally effective are the brief and isolated metaphors, such as Gentleman's "as quickly as an echo follows a sound," that can be found throughout the *Discourse*.

37

As we have seen, humor also figures heavily in Chōmin's style, generally as a means of sharpening characterization or providing a subtle commentary on the speakers' ideas. Gentleman, for example, is fond of alluding to a "god of evolution" whose progress is blocked by reactionary leaders and institutions. It is fitting for the idealistic Gentleman to use such a stirring personification, and it is equally appropriate for Gentleman to insist that the god of evolution loves democracy. But the force of the image is blunted somewhat when Master points out that the Asian god of evolution apparently loves the aristocracy, since there have always been plenty of new aristocrats to replace the old. Gentleman is also fond of basing his arguments on the plain and simple "logic of arithmetic," a phrase characteristic of his search for absolute truths, but its repetition serves only to make his arguments seem more hollow and strident. Gentleman reads history in terms of simple, linear evolution, but, like the "logic of arithmetic," history can yield up any lesson one might wish. Nor is Champion, who later mocks Gentleman's "logic of arithmetic," immune from the logical fallacies that produce much of the book's humor. As Master points out, Champion seems to be a much better analyst of human psychology and behavior than Gentleman. But is he? Champion is incapable of perceiving something as basic and universal as the suffering of soldiers in battle. In fact, he consistently ignores the human side of virtually every issue he discusses. Most significant perhaps is the fact that like Gentleman, Champion is trapped in his own misreading of history. As Master affirms, Champion has learned nothing from the lessons of the past. All he can envision for the future is a continuation of the hoary pattern of attack and retribution.

These are, of course, the kinds of fallacies that anyone could commit in the course of a debate. And this is precisely where the real strengths of the *Discourse* reside. In his masterpiece Chōmin provides a glimpse into the process of political discussion in general as well as a stimulus for a consideration of issues that were being debated by real people in late nineteenth-century Japan. Not only is the outcome problematic, but as in most arguments, the speakers actually agree at more points than they realize. Gentleman and Champion both, for example, want an independent Japan; both want to share in the worldwide expansion of technology and the rising standard of living; both want happiness and prosperity for their people; and both, despite Champion's apparent cynicism, believe that political change can be brought about by careful planning and decisive action. When they disagree, as often as not their disagreement centers on the means to achieve these shared ends.[25] At times, too, the common ground for political debate seems to elude the speakers. Gentleman, for example, is primarily a theorist of democratic government who gradually wanders into the realms of foreign affairs and national defense. Champion, on the other hand, is a warrior whose primary concern is the defense of the country to be achieved through foreign invasion. The debate opens at one side of the domestic-foreign policy spectrum and closes at the other.

The somewhat rambling nature of the debate imitates the way most of us search for answers, and serves to underscore the psychological realism of the *Discourse*. The characters ultimately become as real as the issues, and the enigmatic and indirect phrases they occasionally use remind us that the time and setting of the debate were also very real. Although the ''small Asiatic nation'' and the ''certain large nation'' in either Asia or Africa—Champion claims to have forgotten exactly where it is located—could be easily identified by Chōmin's readers as Japan and China, the indirect allusions most likely reflect once again Chōmin's sensitivity to censorship. If so, his caution was well founded.

39

As we have seen, the new security regulations issued the year the *Discourse* was published forced Chōmin's exile to Osaka, and he was later to face the frequent suspensions of publication already noted. Characteristically, however, Chōmin turns the liability to his advantage in the *Discourse*. The circumspect manner in which the characters speak effectively—and comically—mirrors the difficulty of discussing such issues in light of the constrictions placed upon political debate in Chōmin's day. The very presence of such vague references to the countries involved serves to remind the reader of one of Chōmin's most passionate causes: the freedoms of speech and publishing. In using oblique language, Chōmin also served his own purposes as a writer. Clearly, he was especially committed to getting this book into the hands of the people.

A Note on the Translation

The present translation is based on Nakae Chōmin, *Sansuijin Keirin Mondō*, edited by Kuwabara Takeo and Shimada Kenji (Tokyo: Iwanami Shoten, 1965; 19th printing, 1980), which contains the original text, a modern Japanese translation, notes, and commentary. The translator is indebted to professors Kuwabara and Shimada for permission to use their edition.

In keeping with Japanese usage, Japanese names are written with the family name first and the given name last, except when the person has requested otherwise. We have not translated a few terms, such as units of currency or measurement. They are defined in the notes. In addition, place names, historical allusions, and historical figures that may not be familiar to Western readers are briefly identified in the notes. In our Introduction we have cited books and articles by their original titles. English approximations are given in parentheses.

In the original text, the twenty-one marginal glosses that appear throughout the text are listed as a *mokuji*, a sort of table of contents at the beginning of the book, but this has been omitted from the translation since the entries are not true chapter headings. Instead, they serve as sometimes ironic and often whimsical asides to the narrative. See Kinoshita Junji, "*Sansuijin Keirin Mondō kara Nani o Manabu ka*" (What Do We Learn from "A Discourse by Three Drunkards on Government"?), in *Nakae Chōmin no Sekai* (The World of Nakae Chōmin), ed. Kinoshita Junji and Etō Fumio (Tokyo: Chikuma Shobō, 1977), pp. 10–14.

Notes to the Introduction

1 Matsushima Eiichi, "*Sansuijin Keirin Mondō* no Shironteki Kōsatsu" (A Historical Examination of "A Discourse by Three Drunkards on Government"), in *Nakae Chōmin no Sekai* (The World of Nakae Chōmin), ed. Kinoshita Junji and Etō Fumio (Tokyo: Chikuma Shobō, 1977), p. 213. The present introduction relies on essays in this collection; the chronologies provided in *Nakae Chōmin no Kenkyū* (A Study of Nakae Chōmin), ed. Kuwabara Takeo (Tokyo: Iwanami Shoten, 1966), pp. 351–63, and in Matsunaga Shōzō, *Nakae Chōmin* (Tokyo: Kashiwa Shobō, 1967), pp. 357–69; and the commentary provided by Professor Kuwabara in *Sansuijin Keirin Mondō* (A Discourse by Three Drunkards on Government), ed. Kuwabara Takeo and Shimada Kenji (Tokyo: Iwanami Shoten, 1965; 19th printing, 1980), pp. 255–66.

2 Kuwabara Takeo, "Chōmin e no Sekkin" (An Approach to Chōmin), in *Nakae Chōmin no Sekai*, p. 30.

3 The following biographical sketch summarizes the account of Chōmin's life provided by Professor Kuwabara in his commentary to *Sansuijin Keirin Mondō*, pp. 255–64.

4 Quoted in Kuwabara's commentary, p. 257.

5 Shioda Shōbei, "Jūkyūseiki kara Nijusseiki e: Chōmin to Shūsui" (From the Nineteenth Century to the Twentieth Century: Chōmin and Shūsui), in *Nakae Chōmin no Sekai*, p. 163.

6 Kuwabara, "Chōmin e no Sekkin," in *Nakae Chōmin no Sekai*, pp. 29 and 39.

7 Kinoshita Junji, "*Sansuijin Keirin Mondō* kara Nani o Mana-

buka" (What Do We Learn from "A Discourse by Three Drunkards on Government"?), in *Nakae Chōmin no Sekai*, pp. 7 and 10.

[8] Kinoshita, p. 10; and Kuwabara's commentary, p. 260.

[9] Tōyama Shigeki, "*Sansuijin Keirin Mondō* no Rekishiteki Haikei" (The Historical Background of "A Discourse by Three Drunkards on Government"), in *Nakae Chōmin no Sekai*, p. 45.

[10] Najita, Tetsuo, *Japan: The Intellectual Foundations of Modern Japanese Politics* (Chicago and London: The University of Chicago Press, 1974), p. 96.

[11] Uete Michiari, "Chōmin ni okeru Minken to Kokken" (Popular Rights and State Rights in Chōmin), in *Nakae Chōmin no Sekai*, p. 74.

[12] Uete, pp. 78–79; Hotta Yoshie, "Chishikijin to Taishū: Chōmin no Buntai" (An Intellectual and the Masses: Chōmin's Prose Style), in *Nakae Chōmin no Sekai*, p. 153.

[13] The following discussion of the relation between the *Discourse* and Japanese debate literature is based on Maruyama Masao, "Nihon Shisōshi ni okeru Mondōtai no Keifu" (The Dialogue Form in the History of Japanese Thought), in *Nakae Chōmin no Sekai*, pp. 180–210.

[14] Maruyama, pp. 198–200.

[15] Shioda relates the mingled and overlapping points of view in the work to the turbulent shifts in Japanese political thought in Chōmin's time (p. 177). The open-ended conclusions of the *Discourse* most likely reflect its purpose as a stimulus for political debate; appropriately, Chōmin seems more interested in raising fundamental questions concerning Japan's future than in providing definitive answers (see Uete, p. 97). On the widespread practice of political debate—often with strangers—in Chōmin's Japan, see Etō Fumio, "*Sansuijin Keirin Mondō* e no Shiten" (A Viewpoint Toward "A Discourse by Three Drunkards on Government"), in *Nakae Chōmin no Sekai*, p. 260.

[16] See Uete, pp. 75–77.

[17] Uete, p. 90. For a statement of Chōmin's role as an intellectual activist interested in disseminating Western political theories during the height of the rights movement in Japan, see Uete, p. 71.

[18] Chōmin was impatient with reformers who in his view

moved too quickly or advocated plans that could not be put into practice. Uete has suggested that Master's repudiation of Gentleman's thesis-ridden view of history reflects the fact that Chōmin's initial optimism regarding social change had been shaken by the time he wrote the *Discourse* (pp. 72–73).

[19] See Tōyama, p. 53; and Uete, p. 78.

[20] Shioda, p. 171.

[21] On Chōmin's avoidance of extreme political views, see Uete, pp. 72–77. Hotta suggests that Master's detachment, which reveals his disdain for what Gentleman and Champion are saying, reflects the silent stoicism of the Japanese people who found themselves buffeted about by the political debates of the times (p. 150).

[22] See Uete, p. 96; and Maruyama, pp. 207–9.

[23] Utopian elements in the *Discourse* are treated by Uchida Yoshihiko, "Yūtopia Monogatari to shite no *Sansuijin Keirin Mondō*" ("A Discourse by Three Drunkards on Government" as a Utopian Tale), in *Nakae Chōmin no Sekai*, pp. 242–45.

[24] See Tōyama, p. 53.

[25] See Maruyama, p. 201.

A
Discourse
by
Three Drunkards
on
Government

Japanese relations w/ rest of world:
- developing (w/ West)
- hostile (w/ East)
- self defending/isolated
- minimal (body depi?)

MASTER NANKAI LOVES DRINKING and discussing politics. When he drinks only one or two small bottles of sakè, he is pleasantly intoxicated—his spirits are high and he feels as if he were flying through the universe. Everything he sees and hears delights him; it seems unthinkable that there should be suffering in the world.

When he drinks two or three more bottles, his spirits suddenly soar even higher, and ideas spring up, unrestrained. Although his body remains in his small room, his eyes scan the whole world. They instantly go back a thousand years, or else span the next thousand, charting the direction for the world's course or giving instructions for public policy. At such times, he thinks to himself, "I am the compass for human society. It's a great pity that the world's nearsighted politicians haphazardly take control of the rudder and cause the ship to strike a rock or to be grounded in shallow water, thus bringing calamity upon themselves and others."

Master Nankai does not know the geography of the real world. Even though Master Nankai, the "Master of the Southern Sea," remains physically in the real world, his heart is always climbing the mountain of Hakoya and roaming through the hamlet of

47

Mukayū.* Because of this, the geography and history he discusses have little in common with the geography and history of the real world and there are often, in fact, discrepancies between his world and ours. Of course, in his geography there are cold countries and warm ones, big and powerful nations as well as small and weak ones, civilized societies and barbaric ones. His history, too, contains peace, war, prosperity, and decline. In short, his geography and history sometimes do correspond to the real world.

But if Master Nankai drinks two or three additional bottles, his ears begin to ring and his eyes grow blind. He swings his arms and stamps his feet on the floor. Overcome with excitement, he falls down unconscious. When he comes to his senses after two or three hours' sleep, he has completely forgotten what he said or did while drunk, and seems to have been freed from his possession by the proverbial fox of madness.

From time to time some of Master's acquaintances, or strangers who know of his reputation, visit him in the hope of hearing the strange ideas he expresses while drunk. They come to his house with liquor and food, and drink with him until he is on the verge of becoming totally drunk. Then they deliberately bring up national affairs and amuse themselves by coaxing him into giving his views. Partially aware of this ploy, he thinks to himself, "Next time I talk about national problems, I should carefully write down the main points before I get too drunk. Then later I can look at what I have written, develop my ideas further, and write a short book. Such a book will not only be a pleasure for me but it may also please others. Yes. I'll do it."

* Hakoya (Chinese, Mogushe) is the mountain where *sennin*, legendary hermits endowed with supernatural powers and immortality, were said to live by Zhuangzi (Chuang-tzu), the ancient Chinese philosopher. "Mukayū" (Chinese, Wuheyou) was Zhuangzi's term for Utopia, a realm of nothingness and absolute freedom.

One day, feeling dreary and somewhat depressed after a continuous rain of several days, Master had some liquor brought to him and was drinking alone, until he reached that pleasant state of roaming through the universe. Just at that moment, two visitors arrived with a bottle of European brandy labeled "Golden Axe." Master had never met these people before and did not know their names, but the mere sight of European brandy seemed to increase his intoxication by a third.

An advocate of democracy and an advocate of aggression visit Master Nankai.

One visitor was dressed completely in European style, from top to bottom—right down to his shoes. He had a straight nose, clear eyes, and a slim body. His motions were quick and his speech was distinct. This man appeared to be a philosopher who lived in a room of ideas; he breathed the air of moral principles and marched forward along the straight line of logic. He had disdain for the winding path of reality. The other was a tall man with thick arms. His dark-skinned face, deep-set eyes, outer robe with splashed patterns, and hakama* indicated a man who loved grandeur and cherished adventure, a member of the society of champions who fish for the pleasures of fame with their lives as bait.

When the two were seated and the formal greetings were over, the European brandy was served. As the host and his guests performed the ritual of exchanging their brimming glasses for a series of toasts, Master began to feel expansive. Without bothering to learn their real names, he called one of the guests Mr. Gentleman and the other Mr. Champion. The guests were not offended, but merely

---

* A hakama is a divided skirt worn mainly by men for formal occasions, but also worn by some women (e.g., Shinto priestesses) performing special ceremonies.

kept smiling. After a while, the Gentleman of Western Learning casually began to talk.

"I have long been acquainted with your great fame. I hear that your learning encompasses both the Occident and the Orient, and that your knowledge penetrates the past and the present. I, too, have some personal views on world affairs. I would like your opinion of them.

"Ah, democracy, democracy! Absolute monarchy is stupid. It is unaware of its faults. Constitutionalism is aware of its faults but has corrected only half of them. Democracy, though, is open and frank, without a speck of impurity in its heart.

"Why is it," continued the Gentleman, "that many European nations have not adopted democracy even though they know the three great principles of liberty, equality, and fraternity? Why is it that, against all moral principles and economic laws, these nations maintain standing armies of tens of millions that gnaw at their economies and make their innocent citizens slaughter each other in a vain competition for glory?

"If a small nation which is behind the others in its progress toward civilization were to stand up proudly on the edge of Asia, plunge into the realm of liberty and brotherhood, demolish fortresses, melt down cannon, convert warships into merchant ships, turn soldiers into civilians, devote itself to mastering moral principles, study industrial techniques, and become a true student of philosophy, wouldn't the European nations who take vain pride in their civilization feel ashamed? Suppose, however, those great nations are not only unashamed but also stubborn and villainous, and suppose they impudently invade our country, taking advantage of our disarmament. What could they do if we have not an inch of steel nor a single bullet

National defense is the height of stupidity.

50

about us, but greet them with civility? If you swing a sword to attack the air, nothing happens to the thin, free air no matter how sharp the sword may be. Why don't we become like the air?

"It's like throwing an egg at a rock for a small and powerless nation dealing with a big and powerful one to exert a physical force that is less than one ten-thousandth of its opponent's. Since the opponent takes great pride in his civilization, it cannot be that he lacks the moral principles which are the essence of civilization. Why shouldn't we, a small nation, use as our weapon the intangible moral principles our opponent aspires to but is unable to practice? If we adopt liberty as our army and navy, equality as our fortress, and fraternity as our sword and cannon, who in the world would dare attack us?

"If, on the contrary, we should rely exclusively on fortresses, swords, cannon, and troops, our opponent would also rely on his. As a result, the one with stronger fortifications, sharper swords, more powerful cannon, and larger numbers of troops would necessarily win. This is merely the indisputable logic of arithmetic. Why should we resist such obvious reasoning? Suppose our opponents launch an armed invasion and occupy our country. The land will have to be shared. They exist and we exist; they stay and we stay. What kind of conflict could there be? Suppose they take away our rice fields or our homes, or torment us with heavy taxes. Those who are rich in endurance endure, and those who are not devise their own countermeasures.

"Because we live today in Country A, we are of that nationality. However, if we live in Country B tomorrow, we will be of that nationality. It's just that simple. As long as doomsday is not yet here and the earth, which is the home for our human race, survives, isn't every nation of the world our homestead?

"Truly our opponent lacks civility, while we possess it. He is against reason; we stand for reason. His so-called civilization is nothing but barbarism, and our so-called barbarism is the essence of civilization itself. Even if he gets angry and indulges in violence, what can he do if we smile and adhere to the "way of hu-

Out of a small Asian island a spiritually great nation was born.

manity"?* How would Plato, Mencius, Spencer, Malebranche, Aristotle, or Victor Hugo view us? And what would the watching world say? Regardless of whether or not such a precedent existed before the Deluge, it seems incredible that nobody has tried it since. Why couldn't we ourselves be the precedent?"

Upon hearing these words, the Champion turned to the Gentleman and said, "Have you lost your senses? You're mad. It's insane that a nation of millions of strong men should neither draw its sword nor shoot a single bullet, but instead choose not to resist, letting the invaders pillage. Fortunately I have not yet gone mad. Master Nankai is not crazy, nor are our countrymen. How could we possibly agree with the Gentleman's words—"

Master Nankai interrupted, smiling. "Mr. Champion, wait a little. Let the Gentleman finish his argument."

The Champion smiled, too, and agreed.

The Gentleman continued. "It can be said that those who see themselves as politicians are actually priests who serve the god of political change. If so, they should not only pay attention to what is immediately in front of them, but they should also be mindful of the future. What does this mean? This god of evolution likes to move forward but does not like to retreat. If the path of forward movement is smooth

---

* *Jin* (*ren* in Chinese), variously translated as humanity, benevolence, kindness, or goodness, is one of the fundamental concepts of Confucian thought.

and clean, fine. But even when rocks and stones block the wheels or thick brambles swallow up the horse's hooves, the god of evolution is not disheartened. Undaunted, he rouses himself up even further and lifts his legs to kick away or tread down any obstacles. This god does not flinch even when irrational people fight among themselves and enact the stormy scenes of revolution, ripping open each other's heads, spilling each other's guts, and filling the streets with blood, because he regards such deeds as the natural course of things. Therefore, those politician-priests who devote themselves to this god should always try to remove rocks, stones, and brambles and eliminate any causes for the god's wrath. This is the essential duty of the priest of evolution. What are rocks and stones but systems which oppose the principles of equality? And what are brambles but laws which violate the great principle of liberty?

"If the premier and other ministers in charge of the government during the reign of Charles I of Great Britain or Louis XVI of France had opened their eyes and broadened their minds, if they had quickly perceived the tendency of the times, surmised the future course of history, and possessed the wisdom to clear the path for the god of evolution, they would have prevented upheaval. Great Britain, however, had no previous model to learn from. She was the first to go through the experience and therefore deserves much sympathy for her statesmen's failure to make the necessary provisions and for their subsequent defeat.

"On the other hand, France had no such excuse. She had seen, a century earlier and across the narrow channel, Great Britain's horrible disaster but had learned nothing from it. Instead, she relied on narrow-minded, makeshift policies that wasted time. While the symptoms of upheaval were clearly apparent, France hid her illness and would not call a skilled doctor. Her hesitation aroused suspicion among the common people, and her provocative words and deeds stirred up their emotions. As a result, unprecedented disaster erupted. Blood spilled across the land, and the entire nation was turned into a slaughterhouse. Who is to blame? The god of evolution? Or the priests of the religion of evolution?

"If the premiers and other ministers of an earlier time, when Louis XV was king or in the early years of Louis XVI's reign, had placed themselves decades or even centuries into the future and had made cooperative efforts to remove, one by one, the evils of long-established custom and replace them with fine new plans, France would have needed to take only one more step to adopt democracy and equality by the closing years of Louis XVI's reign. King Louis would have gone to the Parliament with perfect composure, removed his crown and sword, greeted Robespierre and the rest, and with a smile on his calm face said, "Gentlemen, the task lies before us. I am becoming a commoner and will work for our country." Then, accom-

The king of France, Louis XVI, gained happiness.

panied by his wife and children, he would have selected a fertile area of scenic beauty, bought extensive farmland, and lived a comfortable life. And thus he could have left his name to posterity as one who retired from power with grace and dignity.

"I might also add that if France had not had Great Britain as a precedent, no one could severely criticize French premiers and ministers, and my argument would indeed be farfetched or harsh. The fact remains, however, that France had a clear warning but ignored it; front cars overturned but rear ones proceeded without heed. It can be said that the French premiers and ministers of that time deliberately left a disaster to posterity. They were devils blocking the way of the god of evolution. They were criminals who entrapped King Louis."

The Gentleman of Western Learning took another drink and continued. "Carriages like flowing water and horses like swimming dragons rush down the main street of the city where a man in a tall hat and a fashionable suit glides through the crowd as if he were flying, without glancing to either side. Is this man a prime minister with the administrative ability and will to govern the people, a man who executes his duties to assist the sovereign in court? Or is he shrewd by nature, able to catch the drift of the times, buying at a bargain and selling at a high price, and thus becoming a millionaire? Or is he a rare genius who, with his literary excellence or scholarship, can use Cervantes and Pascal as his servants? He is none of these.

"This man's distant ancestor once captured the enemy battle flag and killed the enemy general. For his valor, the ancestor was granted peerage and a fief, and his family has continued to be illustrious to this day. Although his descendant has neither talent nor learning, he receives a rich stipend without performing any work, thanks to the bones of his ancestors which shine from the grave. He drinks good liquor, eats tender meat, and spends his days in a leisurely fashion.

"He is one of those special beings called aristocrats. Ah, as long as hundreds, or even a few dozen, of these beings exist in a nation, even though it has constitutional government and its millions of citizens have obtained their freedom, that freedom is not genuine because the great principle of equality is not exercised completely. We common people work very hard from morning until night and pay part of our earnings as taxes. This may be necessary, but if our taxes feed not only the bureaucrats to whom we have entrusted administration but also these aristocrats who perform no work, then we do not have true freedom.

"Do kings and noblemen possess larger and heavier brains than we? Do they have more gastric juices and blood cells? If we had Dr. Gall* examine their brains, could they be distinguished from ours? And even if they could be, would the distinction be in their favor or in ours? I hear that human beings have a highly developed cerebrum, whereas animals have a highly developed cerebellum. Be that as it may, were kings and noblemen born clad in brocade, and not naked as we were? When they die, don't their bones and flesh decay and turn to dust? If there are even three aristocrats in a nation of one million people, part of the integrity and nobility of the other 999,997 people is diminished on their account. This is the obvious logic of arithmetic. Both we common people and the aristocrats are lumps of flesh made of a combination of a few chemical elements. And yet when we meet, *this* lump of flesh bows low with clasped hands, while *that* lump of flesh remains standing, with only a slight nod of the head. When we talk, *this* lump of flesh shows respect to *that* lump of flesh by calling it 'Sir,' which means 'lord,' or 'Monseigneur,' which also means 'lord.' But what, do you think, does *that* lump of flesh call *this* lump of flesh? . . . —Is this not an extreme affront? Is it not an unbearable shame?

"Here is how the aristocrats think. 'Once upon a time, whatever the year, the month, the day, there was a man of wisdom and virtue. He had talent, intelligence, courage, and ability. For these reasons, this man became a duke, marquis, count, viscount, or baron. Because he was a man of wisdom, virtue, talent, intelligence, courage, and ability, his son, grandson, great-grandson, great-great-grandson, great-great-great-grandson, and his grandsons for ten

* Franz Joseph Gall (1758–1828) was an Austrian doctor of neuroanatomy and psychology. He is best known as the founder of phrenology. Very active as a writer and lecturer, his theories were widely known and discussed in eighteenth- and nineteenth-century Europe.

generations and a hundred generations all possessed wisdom, virtue, talent, intelligence, courage and ability—and all were superior to common people. His descendants hereafter will also necessarily be superior to common people. This is the principle of heredity, not some wild speculation. It follows then that these superior descendants also become dukes, marquises, counts, viscounts, or barons, and place themselves above common men. Their descendants, too, will do the same in the future. This system follows the law of heredity, and so it cannot be unjust. Haven't you ever heard of the theories of Darwin and Haeckel?' . . . —Of course, this entire line of reasoning is utterly ridiculous.

"Millions of us are neither dukes, marquises, counts, viscounts, nor barons. Surely you understand the reason. Our ancestors were neither wise nor virtuous. They were incompetent. Therefore, they could not become dukes, marquises, counts, viscounts, or barons. Nor can we. This is the law of heredity. No matter how badly we want to become dukes, marquises, counts, viscounts, or barons, we can do nothing about the law of heredity. . . . —How ridiculous!

"However, the nature of things includes both a law of regularity and a law of exceptions. For example, even if a father, grandfather, great-grandfather, or any ancestor of ten, a hundred, or ten million generations removed was unwise, unvirtuous, and incompetent and therefore did not become an aristocrat, it can still happen that his child, grandchild, great-grandchild, or descendant of ten, a hundred, a thousand, or ten thousand generations removed turns out to be wise, virtuous, and competent. As a result, such a person is often newly created an aristocrat. This law of exceptions cannot be explained by today's scientific knowledge. When anatomy, physiology, zoology, chemistry, and the other sciences have developed further, the law of exceptions may be clearly explained, and, therefore, some claim that if you want to advocate the great principle of equality, you should first study the law of nature. . . . —Again, how ridiculous!

Making a full-blown defense of Hachi and Kuma.

"Consider, for example, a man with a scarlet carp tattooed on his arms or a blue dragon on his back. He strips himself to the waist and sits with his legs crossed, a proud look on his face. He is a little man living in a humble hut—an uncivilized little man. He already has a name such as Hachi or Kuma, but he is not satisfied with it. He wants instead to be called 'Hachi of the scarlet carp' or 'Kuma of the blue dragon.' Aren't titles such as duke and marquis nothing but invisible tattooing? Since the little man's tattoos are visible, he in his humble hut is deemed uncivilized. The aristocrats in their mansions have invisible tattoos, and are therefore deemed civilized. And even though the aristocrats have their own names, they are given titles as well. Aren't these titles more or less like 'Hachi of the scarlet carp' and 'Kuma of the blue dragon'? Would you reply that the aristocrat has rendered service to the country? But isn't it only natural that a man of his standing should render such service? Doesn't he receive his salary for it? Has he performed a most distinguished service? If so, why shouldn't he be rewarded with extraordinary sums of money and goods? Why should he get tattoos which are no longer fashionable, and thus maim his body, which is a gift from heaven?"

Master Nankai took a drink or two and said, "Mr. Gentleman's remarks are indeed unusual, but they are hopelessly fragmented and incoherent."

The Gentleman of Western Learning said, "Since you are highly knowledgeable and intelligent, please take what is useful out of my jumbled speech, and teach me what I should learn. If I were to follow the rules of logic, I would

58

have to begin with the most obvious point, which would certainly be unworthy of your ears."

Master Nankai replied, "Don't worry about that. I would like you to speak in due order according to the rules of logic. Some day I wish to incorporate your words into a small volume."

Then the Gentleman continued. "Now if you look at the European situation today, four countries—Great Britain, France, Germany, and Russia—are the most powerful, their literatures the most beautiful, their science the most precise, their agriculture, industries, and commerce the most flourishing, and their material goods the most abundant. On the land they maintain tens of thousands of strong soldiers; on the sea they boast several thousand strong battleships. Their forces are like crouching dragons and tigers ready to leap. Since ancient times, we have never seen anything like their prosperity. Of course, the causes that have produced such great power and immense wealth are many and various, but, ultimately, the great principle of liberty was the true foundation of this colossal structure.

"It is true, for example, that Great Britain is rich and powerful thanks to the efforts of her great kings of the past, but the most important reason for her remarkable power is that during the reign of Charles I, waves of liberty swelled and broke the embankment of long-established customs, and the effect of the famous Magna Carta was finally felt.

"France, too, as early as the reign of Louis XIV, enjoyed an unsurpassed reputation for her military power and literary achievements. However, these were nothing more than mold growing in the cellar of a despotic society. France's true strength grew out of the great results of the Revolution of 1789.

"In Germany, ever since Frederick II, the heroic eighteenth-century king of Prussia, showed his military prowess to his neighboring states, the nation has grown increasingly stronger. But until the ideology of the French Revolution reached Germany, the nation was divided into many parts, like a bunch of firewood or fodder in disarray because the rope became untied. However, when Napoleon entered Vienna and Berlin as the commander-in-chief of the Republic with the revolutionary flag fluttering, the German people for the first time breathed the marvelous air of freedom and drank the nourishing milk of brotherhood. Afterwards, the situation changed drastically, public morals reformed completely, and today's prosperity was rapidly achieved.

"As for Russia, her vast territory and large military forces rank first in the world, but her culture and government lag far behind those of the other three nations. Clearly, this is because her despotism is still having its harmful effects.

"All enterprises of human society are like alcohol, and liberty is the yeast. If you try to brew wine or beer without yeast, all the other ingredients, no matter how good they are, will sink to the bottom of the barrel, and your efforts will be in vain. Life in a despotic country is like a brew without ferment: sediments at the bottom of a barrel. Consider, for example, the literature of a despotic country. Occasionally some work appears to be noteworthy, but closer scrutiny reveals that nothing new is produced in a thousand years, nothing unique among ten thousand works. The kinds of phenomena that would ordinarily appeal to an author's sight and hearing are, in these societies, merely sediments at the bottom of a barrel, and the author copies these phenomena with a spirit which is also a sediment. Isn't it only natural then, that there should be no change in the arts?

"Some say that a nation becomes wealthy and powerful

Masters of Chinese studies, please respond here.

60

because it is richly productive. Its productivity is the result of its excellence in learning. If the results of discoveries in physics, chemistry, zoology, botany, and mathematics are applied to commercial industries, time and labor will be saved, and the resulting products will be both more abundant and superior to what is manufactured by hand. This, some say, is the way to enrich a nation. When the nation becomes rich, it will maintain a powerful military force, make strong battleships, and, given the opportunity, send troops to expand its territory and seize lands as far away as Asia and Africa. The nation will then establish markets there by sending colonists. It will buy the raw products of the locality cheaply and sell its manufactured goods at a high price, earning limitless profits. As its industry prospers and its markets expand, its military forces, both on land and at sea, will naturally grow stronger. This growth does not result from adopting the principle of liberty.

"Yet such reasoning only reveals ignorance. It only looks at the surface of things. All human enterprises are interrelated and connected in causal relation. Upon careful observation, one always finds the true cause of any event. A nation's wealth is due to the excellence of its learning, but the excellence of its learning is also due to its wealth. It goes without saying that these two are connected in causal relation. Learning first achieves excellence because human knowledge advances. But once knowledge advances, people naturally open their eyes not only to learning but also to the nature of political systems. Thus, since ancient times, the period in which learning has advanced most dramatically in any nation has also been the period in which political thought has flourished. Learning and political thought are branches, leaves, flowers, and fruit that all grow out of the same trunk, and that trunk is called knowledge.

"Once knowledge advances and political thought

flourishes, the achievement of liberty quickly becomes the goal of all activities. Day and night, a single, unforgettable idea sticks in the minds of scholars, artists, farmers, manufacturers, merchants, and entrepreneurs: they wish to develop their own ideas and attain their own goals without restraint. If those at the top can take a farsighted view of the trends of the times, discern human feelings, outgrow their lust for authority and power, provide leadership for politically active citizens, push open the doors of stale custom and let the air of freedom blow through, then the social machinery will operate to its fullest capacity, decayed elements of society will be naturally eliminated, and fresh nourishment will be absorbed. Scholars will try harder to develop their theories with greater precision, artists will try to improve their conceptions, and people in all walks of life—farmers, manufacturers, and merchants alike—will devote themselves to their professions. From top to bottom, the nation will enjoy the profits of this policy, and an affluent state will emerge. Those ignorant people who can't see beyond the surface of things fail to grasp these far-reaching effects.

"In addition, world affairs always move forward, never backward. This is the immutable law of things, a law already recognized by the philosophers of ancient Greece. For example, when Heraclitus was about to cross the stream and had put one foot into the water, he involuntarily sighed and said, 'The water I have just stepped into is already gone, flowing far away.' He was deeply moved by this law. Of course, at that time empiricism was not fully developed and science was still primitive. Therefore, expressions such as that of Heraclitus seemed exaggerated to many people.

"In the eighteenth century, the Frenchmen Diderot and the Marquis de Condorcet affirmed that this law of evolution was constantly in operation, especially in human society. Then Lamarck, famed zoologist and botanist, advanced for the first time the theory that every species changes from generation to generation and that none remains the same forever. Since then, Goethe of Germany and Geoffroy of France developed Lamarck's theory further. The Englishman Darwin had wide learning and deep knowledge. His experimental method was more precise and he discovered the law of mutation, by which characteristics are transmitted from one generation to the next. After he investigated the origin of the human species and exposed its secrets, the great theory of evolution, of which Lamarck and other scholars had had a vague intimation, saw light in the world. Thus, there can no longer be any doubt that all things in the universe—from the sun, moon, stars, rivers, seas, mountains, animals, plants, and insects, to societies, human affairs, political systems, and the literary art—are controlled by this principle of evolution. All things move forward gradually, but steadily and unceasingly.

"Let me discuss this point a little further. 'Evolution' means to proceed from an imperfect to a perfect shape, to change from an impure to a pure form. Generally speaking, it means that what begins ugly becomes beautiful in the end, and that what is bad becomes good. Consider animals, for example. At first a few elements mingle together to form a smooth and sticky lump. This lump has no specialized structures, such as digestive or respiratory organs, but only expands or contracts like a worm, absorbs food through its body surface, discharges residue through its back, and thus maintains its life. Later, the stimulus of external elements combines with the ability of cellular tissues to grow. As a result, the lungs and stomach are formed. Because of evolution, each animal is equipped with such marvelous and sensitive organs as the brain, the spine, and the nervous system. This is the manifestation of the law of evolution in the animal world.

63

"The same is true with us. In the beginning, human beings lived in caves or in the field, gathered food and water, and copulated without marriage vows. Later they began building houses by laying down wood or piling stones. They also began hunting and farming. Men labored outdoors and women managed indoors. They raised children and nurtured grandchildren. This is the manifestation of the law of evolution in the human world.

"Consider the evolution of government. In the earliest societies, we find no political system at all. The strong control the weak and the clever deceive the stupid. He who intimidates and overpowers others becomes the master and he who fears and submits to others becomes the slave. One man falls and another man rises, and there is complete chaos, no unity. Gradually, when people become weary of wars and conflicts and begin wishing for a peaceful life, a man of talent and virtue appears, fires the hearts of the people, and becomes their sovereign. Or, a man of power and cunning entices the masses and takes it upon himself to be their sovereign. Having accomplished that, he issues laws to seek immediate peace and order. This is called absolute monarchy, the first step in the law of political evolution.

"In this system there exists a certain intangible tool that unites the two parties—the ruler and the ruled, the government and the people—into an inseparable whole. Because of this, absolute monarchy represents an advance by one stage over the earlier state, wherein tangible physical force permanently maintained a master-slave relationship that should have been merely temporary. What is this intangible tool? It is the loyalty between sovereign and subject. This loyalty is not necessarily artificial, for it is based on a combination of benevolence and gratitude. The sovereign bestows his benevolence upon his subjects and the people offer their gratitude to their sovereign. Therefore, with an

64

increase of benevolence from above and gratitude from below, the loyalty between sovereign and subject becomes stronger and the relationship between ruler and ruled is solidified. In China, the well-governed periods at the beginnings of the Xia, Shang, Zhou, Han, and Tang dynasties are good examples of this.*

"But this system contains one persistent germ of a disease. The gratitude that the subjects offer up is merely a reflection of the benevolence that the sovereign bestows downward. Therefore, if the sovereign's benevolence diminishes by ten percent, the people's gratitude also diminishes by ten percent. This reaction occurs as quickly as an echo follows a sound. Now the degree of the sovereign's benevolence is primarily determined by his personal character. Unfortunately, if the sovereign is an inferior man by nature nothing good will result, no matter how hard his subjects may try to advise and guide him. The loyalty between sovereign and subject ceases to exist, and disorder and ruin will result. The Xia, Shang, Zhou, Han, and Tang dynasties ended in just this way.

"Now let us suppose that by the grace of heaven succeeding sovereigns have consistently superior qualities and bestow more and more benevolence on their subjects, and that in turn their subjects offer more and more gratitude to their ruler, so that the nation is able to maintain unrestrained peace and happiness for tens of thousands of years. Even in this case another and even more dreadful source of disease arises. What is it? People support themselves by their labor, submit part of their income to the government,

* The legendary Xia dynasty was thought to have extended from c. 2100 to 1600 B.C.; the Shang (also called Yin) extended from 1766 to 1122 or 1027 B.C.; the Zhou from 1122 or 1027 to 221 B.C.; the Han from 206 B.C. to A.D. 220; and the Tang from 618 to 907. All of these dynasties are known for their long reigns, well-governed at the start but gradually disintegrating into tyranny and disorder.

and consequently feel that their duties to the state are completely fulfilled. Thus they grow indifferent. Scholars think only of perfecting their writings. Artists think only of polishing their skills. Those engaged in agriculture, industry, and commerce think only of high profit and become indifferent to everything else. Under these circumstances, the function of the brain gradually shrinks, and the complete human being is reduced to a mere digester of food. In other words, the scholar's writings, the artist's skills, the works of those engaged in agriculture, industry, and commerce eventually become the sediments I mentioned earlier, sediments at the bottom of a barrel, without vitality or change. The entire nation becomes a mere lump of slimy, jellylike flesh.

"Why did our ancestors willingly submit themselves to a sovereign's rule, entrust every matter to him, and obey his orders? There is only one reason: they were ignorant and could not support themselves by being their own masters. Thus they abandoned their rights for the time being as a temporary expedient, hoping that in later generations, when their descendants' knowledge had gradually increased, they could regain their independence. No such agreement was explicitly made between ruler and subject in the beginning, but when we consider the deeper meaning of monarchy, these are the implications of the relationship between ruler and ruled. Owing to long-established custom, however, the sovereign who was entrusted with our ancestors' rights as a temporary expedient would not return them to us, and instead insisted that they were his to begin with. Thus, as I have said, the system of absolute monarchy is blindly unaware of its own insolence.

"Read the history of all the nations of the world and study their political journeys for the hundreds or thousands of years since their founding. Except for the barbaric tribes of Africa, all these nations share one characteristic: they all emerged from the period of chaos and lawlessness and entered the stage of monarchy, which is the first step in the law of evolution. Unfortunately, the peoples of Asia have not been able to get beyond this stage. European nations came out of this first stage and entered the second, some as early as the seventeenth century and others in the eighteenth. This is the main reason why the Orient and the Occident differ in their progress in civilization.

"O, law of evolution! Law of evolution! Ceaseless progress is your true nature. Once you drove your children out of the wilderness of chaos and disorder into the narrow valley of despotism, where you let them rest for a while until they gained strength. After that, you drove your children out of the valley and made them climb up to the top of the wide hill of constitutionalism, where you let them dry their eyes and breathe freely. When they turn their eyes upward, they see the green trees soaring into the sky, a trailing mist of clouds, and birds singing harmoniously. This is the high peak of democracy, with a view unparalleled in the world. Later, I shall explain more fully the superior vistas of this peak.

"O, law of evolution! When Greece and Rome were in their prime, a free system seemed to have developed considerably, but because there remained the blemish of slavery, you did not wish to let your light shine completely. In modern times, Great Britain was the first nation to serve and worship you. Ever since you favored the Anglo-Saxon race with your presence, Englishmen have scrambled for the ideal, rousing their spirits and waving the banner of freedom, charging at the enemy and shouting in loud voices. Once the blood of Charles I spouted over the execution ground, the grand words of the illustrious Magna Carta began to illuminate the world. O, law of evolution! You are by nature gentle and do not like to kill people. But when human emotions are aroused, even you cannot

67

subdue them. When you encounter the anxious conservatism that adheres to the old, fears the new, and blocks the road with bigotry, you have no choice but to kick over the obstacle and move on. Who can blame you?

"And what is the second stage in the law of evolution? Nothing other than constitutionalism."

Emptying another glass, the Gentleman of Western Learning turned to Master Nankai and said,

"If I continue to speak such obvious truths, you may become ill."

Master Nankai said, "No, no. In European nations, your discourse may be commonplace, but here in Asia your ideas are still fresh. Please don't tire of speaking, but continue your argument to its conclusion."

Encouraged, the Gentleman of Western Learning continued. "In constitutionalism, too, as in absolute monarchy, the sovereign who calls himself "emperor" or "king" holds a hereditary position and stands sternly above his people. He is surrounded by the aristocrats—dukes, marquises, counts, viscounts, or barons—who are also hereditary and protect the sovereign. Up to this point, this system is no different from despotism.

"In constitutional nations, however, the system of aristocracy often signifies merely the honor of the titled person and his family, and the benefit attached to the title is simply that he is eligible for a seat in the Upper House of Parliament. If his lands and wealth are extensive, it is a result of his business management, and he is no different from those farmers, artisans, and merchants who have acquired wealth through good husbandry. Aristocrats in constitutional states are thus quite different from those in despotic states, where they suck the blood of the commoners and accumulate their personal wealth without working. This is yet another reason why constitutionalism is superior to despotism.

"Furthermore, only when a nation progresses beyond despotism and enters constitutionalism can human beings realize their individuality. What does this mean? The right to participate in government, to own personal property, and to choose one's livelihood; the rights to freedom of religion, freedom of speech, freedom of the press, and freedom of assembly—these are the kinds of rights which all human beings should possess, and only when they do possess these rights are they worthy of being called human. Suppose a human being has a head but no hands, or hands but no legs. This person is clearly physically handicapped. When a human being does not have the rights I've mentioned, he is by necessity spiritually handicapped.

"In a constitutional system, citizens vote to elect men of high reputation as their representatives and entrust them with the supreme power of legislation in a body called 'Parliament.' The Parliament is where the will of the citizens of the entire nation resides. The premier and other cabinet ministers are merely subordinate to the Parliament and take partial charge of various kinds of business. The legislative power, or the Parliament, is the master who delegates the business of government on behalf of the people. The premier and other ministers, who represent the executive power, are mere employees who perform the business entrusted to them. The citizens have the right to elect their representatives and to supervise government affairs. It goes without saying, also, that the citizens have other natural rights.

"Considering what I have said so far, isn't it clear that there is considerable distance between the first step in the law of political evolution, absolute monarchy, and the second step, constitutional government? In nations under absolute monarchy, the only people who can be called human beings are the royal family and the aristocrats. The remaining millions become spiritually handicapped, mere processors of food. Even if we citizens save money by our hard labor, the sovereign will arbitrarily issue laws and ordinances to collect taxes if his money reserves should dwindle or if he should have an unexpected expense. The sovereign will not indicate whether or not the taxes will benefit us. Such taxation is no different from directly stealing our money from us. Where is the right of private property? Also, when we wish to pursue the business of our choice, many strict regulations prevent us from choosing freely. This restriction is no different from directly restraining our bodies. Where is the right to pursue a trade? In religious matters, the ruler oppresses our hearts and minds; to govern our speech, he locks our lips and tongues. If we try to publish, he binds our hands and arms; if we try to band together to achieve our goals, he suppresses our emotions and our desires. Under these circumstances, we are like the grass growing on the wayside. Even if the grass takes root, new shoots will be stepped on, pulled out, or allowed to wither prematurely. Where is freedom?

How enviable!
How pitiable!
"Furthermore, in despotic nations, the career of a government official is highly valued while the career of an ordinary citizen is despised. Of course government officials whose names are entered on the government registers must receive the favors of their ruler if they wish to achieve success, but merchants engaged in private business must rely on favors as well if they wish to expand their businesses and to be successful. Those engaged in farming, industry, commerce, or any other business who own large farms, big shops, or fine factories and employ many workers have without exception received, either openly or covertly, the life-giving drops of the ruler's private blessings. This is evident. You don't even have to ask about it.

"Whoever prides himself on his prowess as a writer or on his creativity as an artist or craftsman may appear insulated

70

from this world of power, but if you observe carefully, this is not the case. Unless someone actually becomes a government official, secretly asks the guard at the gate to arrange an audience with the sovereign, smiles like a sycophant, flatters like a buffoon, or sells his favors to buy someone else's love, he cannot write magnificent sentences, compose beautiful verses, or create marvelous art. Ah, the ruler is like the heart. Even healthy hair and teeth will instantly fall out if the blood does not nurture them.

"If such is the case of the artist and the craftsman, what about government officials? The old saying describes their behavior perfectly: 'Government officials receive their appointments in public from the court, but pay their gratitude privately; in the day they are arrogant, but in the evening they beg for pity.' Isn't it the essence of honor to have respect and regard for one's self and not to be servile? Look at the condition of government officials. Do they have self-esteem and a sense of honor? If they had these things, they would be unable to remain in their profession for even one day. If they express honest protest in the morning, they will receive a notice of dismissal in the evening. If they do not receive their salary, their families cannot subsist. It is better for them to remain silent with their heads bowed, enjoying the pleasures of family life, eating fresh food, and wearing light, warm clothing, than to die of cold and hunger and bring the same fate upon their families. Isn't this the simplest rule of logic? What's the use of noisily imitating men who were once influential but have lost their popularity? . . . 'Once you were in a certain government office and held a certain position; later you were in another government office and held another position. You have been swimming in the sea of government bureaucracy for a long time. Why is it that you continue to be so stubborn and childish?'

"Now one thing about people living under despotic

71

government makes us burst out laughing—an absurd phenomenon but a real one, and, psychologically, necessary and reasonable. What is it? These people, these flatterers, glib talkers, and smart alecks, are unashamed of their servitude and are most arrogant when dealing with a stranger of the same or lower rank. They will stand up, thrust out their chests, and turn their faces to the side, fixing a suspicious stare on the stranger. They will make him utter ten words, while they answer with only a nod of the head. Even if he bursts out laughing, they will only smile. There is not a speck of real honesty in them. They probably behave this way because they wish to appear solemn and dignified, but they are by nature haughty. This haughtiness has no resemblance to the servitude they show to a superior. They behave like two completely different people.

"But such a person is not two different people. To say and do what one pleases and to behave freely—these are basic to human nature. And yet, these functionaries take pains to suppress their feelings and not to reveal themselves easily. At first this is an effort, but after they have practiced these restraints for a long time, they reach the stage where they can skillfully sell their favors or flatter superiors without conscious effort. Even so, human nature cannot be erased completely. Therefore, when they have a chance to show their feelings without any harmful effects, they become arrogant and thus compensate for their everyday servitude. Such is the natural psychological tendency of a human being. Some Westerners say that the citizens of a free nation are gentle and do not quarrel with others, but that those in a despotic country are arrogant and domineering. Clearly, the saying is true.

"In view of what I've said, we can see that freedom not only benefits the citizen's life, livelihood, and business, but it also undeniably ennobles the human heart. Ah, freedom! If I abandon you, what else can I embrace?

72

"But if we consider further the law of political evolution, we see that a democratic system cannot realize its ultimate perfection by freedom alone; in addition, equality is needed to fulfill its potential. Unless all the people's rights are intact and unless there is no discrepancy in how many rights they have, it is inevitable that those with more rights will have more freedom and that those with fewer rights will have less freedom. Therefore, equality and freedom are the supreme rules of the system. In a constitutional nation, the presence of the sovereign and the aristocrats creates among its citizens one entity more noble than the rest and thus distinguished from the others, exposing the nation's lack of the great principle of equality. A constitutional nation knows that freedom is the principle which must necessarily be followed; indeed, it has established the constitution and instituted laws to protect the people's rights and to prohibit the violation of these rights. In this respect, the nation has achieved its goal of liberty. However, the nation has also chosen a handful of people, given them the invisible tattoos of titles, and placed them above the others. The nation has thus damaged the cause of equality but is unable to remedy the problem. Surely the law of political evolution will not remain in this stage forever. Therefore, I say that constitutionalism knows its mistakes but has corrected only half of them.

"In the seventeenth century Great Britain established the principle of freedom before any other nation and greatly enhanced her national prestige. But since the British are by nature calm and steady, they did not wish to get rid of all established customs at once and enter a completely new road. Instead, even to this day, they maintain a monarchy. But if you study the British government carefully, its so-called monarchy is actually not much different from democracy. Except for two or three prerogatives of the sovereign, the main difference between him and the president of a democratic nation is that his office is hereditary. For this reason, when Western scholars discuss politics, they generally include Great Britain among democratic nations and do not distinguish her from the United States, France, or Switzerland.

"But as the saying goes, 'The name is secondary to the substance.'* It's fine to have both the substance and the name, but it goes against reason to have the name without the substance. In Great Britain, with the hereditary royal family standing regally above the entire nation and with the institution of five hereditary aristocratic titles, the great cause of equality is not completely achieved. Therefore, many Englishmen with progressive ideas and well-developed moral principles strongly desire to go a step further and to adopt democracy by combining the principle of freedom with the principle of equality. This is no surprise. Compared to the other animals, human beings are the quickest to follow the law of evolution; and scholars and thinkers are quicker to follow the law of evolution than the rest of us. And democracy, of course, is the third stage in the law of political evolution.

"Constitutionalism is nearly perfect, but it has some elements that cause a slight headache. I don't understand why. And even though I don't, I do have a headache now. It is as if I am wearing a heavy iron hat on my head on a day when a hot wind blows, while I have a light, unlined garment on my body. Democracy! Democracy! Above your head is the blue sky; beneath your feet is the earth. Your heart is refreshed and your spirits are high. You encompass eternity— we know not how many hundred million years into the past or into the future. In you is no beginning or ending. And you are as vast as the universe itself—we know not how many

* This is a quotation from the *Zhuangzi* (*Chuang-tzu*), Book 1 (*Xiaoyaoyu*).

74

hundred million miles to the right or to the left you extend. In you exists neither inside nor outside.

"All who possess mind and body are equally human. What is the difference between the Europeans and the Asians, much less between the British, the French, the Germans, and the Russians, or between the Indians, Chinese, and Ryukyuans?* Today we invariably refer to Great Britain, Russia, or Germany, but these are merely the names of the sovereigns' properties. If, however, sovereignty rests with the people and there is no other ruler, a country's name simply designates a certain part of the surface of the earth. Therefore, to say that one is a citizen of a certain country ultimately means that one lives in that part of the earth. There are no borders between oneself and others and there arises no hostility. Nations with a single master, however, are named after the master's house. In such a nation, to say that one is of a certain nationality means, ultimately, that one is a subject of that nation's king. In other words, a boundary exists between oneself and others. This slicing up of the various parts of the earth, causing divisions among its inhabitants, is the course of monarchy. Democracy! Democracy! Country A or B is merely a division made for the sake of convenience in naming various parts of the earth. These names were not meant to build walls among its inhabitants. Democracy creates a single, large, complete circle embracing the entire earth by bringing together the wisdom and love of the people of the world.

"Constitutionalism is not bad but democracy is better." Constitutionalism is spring with a faint touch of frost or

* The Ryukyu Islands, which include Okinawa, were under the rule of both Japan and China until 1871, when Japan arbitrarily annexed them. China refused to recognize the annexation until after Japan's invasion of Taiwan in 1874. Chōmin most likely has these events in mind in referring to the Ryukyuans.

snow; democracy is summer with no trace of frost or snow. As the Chinese might put it, constitutionalism is a wise man, but democracy is a sacred man. Or, in the phrasing of India, constitutionalism is a bodhisattva, but democracy is a buddha. Constitutionalism is to be respected, but democracy loved. Constitutionalism is an inn from which we have to depart sooner or later. It is only the weak or crippled who cannot leave. Democracy is a final home. What a restful feeling to return home after a long journey!

Laughing, the author answers, "This passage is a poor imitation of Chinese writing."

"France took the path of freedom a little later than Great Britain. It was truly commendable that France proceeded to democracy in one leap. The British are rational and the French emotional; the British are calm and the French turbulent. Once the British have taken the path of progress, they no longer waver. The French, on the other hand, are quick to move forward but just as quick to retreat. Ah, but have the French really retreated? They decapitated Louis XVI, scooped up his warm blood, and poured it over the heads of the other European kings. Without clothing, shoes, weapons, or food, Frenchmen dashed forward with increasing vigor, each bearing a great halo of equality over his head. No enemy bullet or enemy sword could harm them. But it was madness to try to overturn existing systems at a single stroke and to replace them with the principle of equality.

"Napoleon was successful a hundred times in his hundred expeditions and won a thousand victories in his thousand battles. None of the forces of Prussia, Austria, Russia, or Great Britain could oppose him. This was partly because his military strategies were superb, but it was also because Frenchmen at that time were intoxicated with the mad fever called equality and their physical and mental energy became almost superhuman. Despite their fervor, however, the French suddenly forgot the powerful aura of equality, became blinded by the colors of Napoleon's banner, and drove away the celestial maid of democracy. They nurtured a vicious, fierce tiger called imperialism, scrambled to become its victims, and allowed themselves to regress a hundred years. Thus the structure of French society quickly lost its underlying logic.

"This reveals the turbulence of the French spirit. The spirit of Great Britain, logical and coherent, is that of an accomplished man. But the French spirit is that of a genius; it ignores logic and soars dramatically. Later, the French overthrew Louis Philippe, Charles X, and Napoleon III, and thus democratic government reached a new stage. Such incessant fluctuations are the logic of the French style. Her life is like her writing. From the beginning to the end, rapid shifts make the reader in turn delighted or distressed, joyful or angry. While Great Britain is a school textbook, France is a drama. Great Britain is a framed painting by Raphael; France is a mural by Michelangelo. Great Britain is Du Fu's poetry, strict and formal; France is Li Bo's more relaxed and flowing verse. Great Britain is the rigid General Cheng Bushi; France is the more pliable General Li Guang.* And what about Germany? She practices politics but is not yet a nation with a political theory."

Suddenly the Gentleman of Western Learning interrupted himself and said, "I've gotten carried away. I'm starting to

---

* Du Fu (712–70) was a Chinese Confucian poet, noted for his skill in writing the tightly regulated verse form known as *lu shi*. Li Bo (701–62) was a Chinese Taoist poet who wrote mainly "old style," or *gu shi*, verse, which did not follow such strict rules.

Cheng Bushi and Li Guang were military figures of the early Han period. Cheng Bushi was said to be more strict in his adherence to military codes and procedures.

77

babble, and I've lost the thread of my argument. Master, please forgive me.''

The Gentleman began again, this time in a louder voice. ''If a nation possesses a vast territory, keeps a million strong soldiers, maintains a hundred or a thousand well-built battleships, has a large and well-to-do population and is rich in agricultural products, then, of course, such a nation finds it easy to rely on its wealth and strength and to scorn the other nations. But if a nation possesses a small territory and a small population, it has nothing to rely upon for protection but moral principles. If it has an army of only for a little over a hundred thousand men and only a dozen or so battleships and tries to expand its forces extensively to match those of other powerful nations, it will face financial difficulty, be forced to impose heavy taxes, and inevitably incur the resentment of its people. Even if more farm land is reclaimed and agricultural output is increased, a nation with little territory cannot expand itself suddenly or increase its agricultural productivity at will, since there is a limit to what its land can yield. Though the nation tries to develop its industries and profit from the sale of machinery or crafts, and even if its industrial productivity should increase, as long as the nation cannot find buyers for its goods, its efforts will be of no use.

''Consider the economic conditions of Europe. Great Britain has taken possession of India and, using it as a base, has made a foolproof policy of invading all the territories of Asia, Africa, and America, sending immigrants there and fattening herself. France took Algeria in Africa, Saigon in India, and Annam in China.* Others have done the same.

---

* The geographical error that places Saigon in India occurs in the original. Professors Kuwabara and Shimada suggest Pondicherry instead of Saigon as a geographically correct reading (p. 226). When Chōmin refers to ''Annam in China'' he evidently uses ''China'' in its broadest geographical sense, encompassing Indochina as well as China.

Although there are differences in the size of the occupied territories or in the degree of influence these nations possess, each of these countries holds territory it invaded and occupied. Nor is there a nation which has not established a policy to open up markets for its own products. It is either stupidity or insanity for a small, insignificant nation to send its scant army of a hundred thousand men and its fleet of ten to a hundred battleships to invade a far-off foreign land to enhance the flow of its economy. Since a nation has no alternative but to protect itself and try to achieve self-sufficiency, it must come up with a policy for that purpose.

"Let me tell you what this policy should be. Such a nation should establish a system of democracy and equality, return to its citizens control over their own lives, demolish fortresses, cease all military preparations, and show other nations that it has no intention to commit murder. The nation should also indicate that it suspects no other nations of such intentions either, and convert the entire country into a flourishing garden of moral principles and scholarship. The nation should establish a unicameral legislature and strive to preserve the people's spirit and unity. It should let all adults, poor or rich, male or female—unless they are retarded, insane, or otherwise troublesome in their behavior—have voting rights and eligibility for election as independent human beings. Local government officials, from the prefectural governor down to the village chief, should all be elected in order to eliminate their need to seek favors from higher government officials. The judges should also be elected for the same reason. This nation should build many tuition-free schools and make all the citizens aspire to become gentlemen through learning. It should abolish the death penalty and demolish the gallows, a mere tool for legal cruelty. It should repeal protective tariffs so as to remove the ills of economic jealousy, strike down all laws regulating speech, publication, and freedom of association, and, unless they corrupt public morals or incite riots, give freedom of speech to those who argue, freedom of hearing to those who listen, freedom of the hand to those who write, freedom of the eyes to those who read, and freedom of the feet to those who gather. These are the main points. Let me discuss the details separately.

"Everybody loves and yearns for such a garden of moral principles. No one would have the heart to despoil it. Everyone cultivates the farm of learning and benefits from its produce; nobody wishes to plunder it. But we must be allowed to try out these principles. We can stop the experiment if the result is not favorable; there should be no harm in that. Take chemists, for example. If they discover anything new, they go to the laboratory and conduct experiments. I want to make this small Asian nation a laboratory for democracy, equality, moral principles, and learning. We might be able to distill the world's most precious and most beloved compound: world peace and universal happiness. We may become a Priestley or Lavoisier of sociological experimentation. This is what my policy would be.

"The god of evolution, who always watches over us from above, may give vent to his wrath frequently or rarely, once every hundred years or every thousand years. When he gets angry frequently, his anger may not be very fierce, but if he gets angry once every thousand years, his fury will be devastating. Why? We human beings are so short-sighted that when the god of evolution seems mild and speaks with a gentle voice, we do not try to remove the rocks of inequality or the brambles of tyranny which block his road. Still, when the god comes to these spots, he will release his anger and push on. This is inevitable.

"Therefore, the politician who functions as a priest in the service of this god should calculate how often this god has shown his anger in his country. If the god's anger has been infrequent, then the politician-priest should make strenuous efforts at reform. If he does not pay enough attention to such signs, half a century or several centuries later his sovereign will inevitably become another Charles I of Great Britain or Louis XVI of France, and the sovereign and his subjects will both suffer and become a laughing stock for posterity. The politician-priest should take note. Even if it is impossible to bring about radical reform, why does he add more rocks and let more brambles obstruct the path of the god of evolution, who will surely come by sooner or later? How can anyone deliberately incur such wrath?

"Some reply that although democracy is a truly reasonable system, it is extremely difficult to put into practice. Unless learning is advanced and public morals are completely reformed, democracy will only invite confusion, they say. In a democracy, a president heads the executive functions of government. But since he holds office through the votes of the masses, his authority is far different from that of a king or an emperor. If, for example, a powerful and ambitious man with imprudent intentions should become president, the unity of government and people will shatter and the entire nation will inevitably fall into utter chaos. It is quite natural to desire a position of honor and respect, and, even though the position of the president is obtained through election, it is nonetheless the most respected and honored position in the nation. Therefore, in a democratic country, those with a strong will seek the presidency, using every possible means to attain mass popularity. The frenetic and unavoidable result is that everyone is trying to get ahead of his competitors, which some claim is the common ill of all democratic countries.

"Constitutionalism, however, is different, some say. The fact that there is a permanent sovereign is sufficient to control any imprudent ambition. In addition, since there exists a sacred and inviolable constitution, even those in the highest ranks, such as princes, generals, and cabinet ministers, cannot behave as they please, and thus the citizens can maintain their freedom. In other words, a constitutional monarchy lies between absolute monarchy and democracy. Constitutionalism resembles despotism in that the sacred position of the sovereign can control imprudent ambition. And constitutionalism resembles democracy in that the citizens are free. Therefore, constitutionalism supposedly combines the merits of the other two systems while containing none of their flaws. Montesquieu in *De l'Esprit des Lois* and John Stuart Mill in *Representative Government* maintain that the political system must be appropriate to the stage of development of the people.

"But such an argument is the cliché of an old man. It hinders progress in the world. The argument may appear sound, but in reality it is not. Look at those governments which are presently democratic. Are the citizens of the United States, France, and Switzerland all gentlemen? Are their public morals pure and flawless? Of course not. But do their presidential elections always produce civil unrest? No, they don't. Are the citizens afraid that powerful and ambitious men always hold imprudent desires? No, they aren't.

"Let's carry our argument one step further. If the citizens of a constitutional monarchy can enjoy peace and order solely because of their sacred sovereign, then the happy result of their peace and order is not obtained by their own right to freedom, but by the favor of the sovereign. But like others, the sovereign is human. And even though he and his subjects belong to the same human race, the citizens of the constitutional monarchy cannot enjoy their own rights but by the grace of someone else. Isn't that truly shameful?"

The Gentleman continued. "Democracy is necessary for

82

abolishing war, promoting peace, and making all the nations on earth one family. The theory that all nations should give up war and promote peace was first advocated by the Frenchman Abbé de Saint-Pierre in the eighteenth century. At that time, very few people agreed with his idea, and many said that it could not be put into practice. Some went so far as to ridicule him as a high-minded ideologue. Even Voltaire, a man of uncommon intelligence who was deeply interested in the progress of society, tried to appear clever by making some derisive remarks concerning Saint-Pierre's theory. Only Jean Jacques Rousseau, wielding his mighty pen, completely agreed with the theory, and praised Saint-Pierre's book as 'indispensable.' Later, Kant built upon Saint-Pierre's theory and wrote a book entitled *Zum ewigen Frieden,* which advocated the necessity of abolishing war and promoting friendly relations. According to Kant, 'Even if we grant the contention that the desire for fame and love of victory cannot be removed from human beings and that the realization of peace is impossible in our actual world, as long as we value moral principles, we must make every effort to move forward toward that realm. This, and nothing else, is the responsibility of human beings.'

"Of course, as a modern scholar, I find one point unsatisfying in Saint-Pierre's theory—the question of how to abolish war. From the beginning of history, there have always been many reasons why nations begin wars and attack each other, but a careful study shows that the desire for glory and the love of military power on the part of the sovereign, the general, and the premier are always the source of disaster. Therefore, unless all nations adopt democracy, there is no hope for abolishing war. Saint-Pierre did not take this point into consideration, nor did he pay the slightest attention to the actual conditions of every nation of his time. Instead, he simply accepted the age-old system of diplomacy without attempting to make substantial reforms; relying exclusively on such minor details as treaties and alliances, he tried to realize peace. How is that possible, when sovereigns, generals, and premiers are concerned only with the relative strength of their forces? If their opponents are stronger, they have no choice but to make a temporary peace and conclude a treaty. But once their nation has become wealthy and their troops strong, their uncontrollable ambitions cannot be checked, even if they have signed a thousand treaties.

"Recently, the French philosopher Émile Acollas placed international law under the heading of moral principles rather than under the law in his study of legal classification. According to Acollas, every law should always have an official who administers and enforces it; moreover, if any-one violates the law, he must always be punished. If this is not the case, the law is not the true law. On the other hand, moral principles reside in the conscience of people, wheth-er or not such principles are observed. The same can be said concerning so-called international law. No office en-forces it and no official administers penalties. Therefore, it is impossible to regard international law as true law.

"In discussing the kinds of war among nations, Acollas asserts that there are four causes of war: a dispute over the succession of the throne; a dispute over religion; a racial dispute; or a dispute over trade. Of the four, religious dis-putes and racial disputes have mostly disappeared in recent years and are no longer very divisive. But many nations still resort to military acts in their struggle to obtain key terri-tories or markets for their products, or in their disputes over the royal succession. And if we investigate further, we find that whatever the cause, sovereigns and premiers have often decided to use force on the slightest pretext in order to pursue their own glory. In democratic nations, however, the law of liberty, the principle of equality, and the feeling of brotherhood form the three-part basis of society. Dem-

84

ocratic nations try to surpass other nations only in terms of developing learning and economic wealth. In short, despotic nations attempt to triumph over their neighbors by means of tangible force, and democratic nations by means of intangible ideas.

"Since Saint-Pierre first expressed his theory of world peace, Rousseau has praised it and Kant has developed it so that it has come to have the rational qualities suitable for a philosophy. Let me cite some of Kant's remarks.

"First of all, Kant says that if all nations wish to abolish war and achieve the benefits of peace, they must adopt democracy. When nations become democratic, citizens are no longer the possessions of their sovereign but become their own masters. Once they gain their independence, what could cause them willingly to kill each other? When two nations attack each other, who carries the burden of all the disasters caused by war? It's the citizens who bear arms and fight. It's the citizens who pay for military expenditures. And it's the citizens whose homes are burned, whose farms are trampled underfoot, and who suffer the damage. After the war is over, it is also the citizens who are asked to buy government bonds and to pay for reconstruction programs. Moreover, the government bonds of this kind can never be completely redeemed, because once a war is fought, misfortune continues and hostility deepens, so that even if peace is achieved temporarily, another war will inevitably soon follow. Given this fact, is there any reason why citizens would voluntarily make war?

"Kant also explains the connection between monarchy and war. The sovereign owns the nation; he is not one of its citizens. Therefore, the sovereign has no concern over shedding citizens' blood and spending their wealth. Why? While the troops clash, the shells kill, the bullets maim, the entrails of soldiers mingle with the soil, and their blood seeps into the fields, the sovereign hunts in the royal hunting ground or feasts at the palace, just as on any ordinary day. When he sends the troops off he cites a grand cause for war, but in reality he is merely pursuing his own glory at the expense of his subjects' lives and property. War is, after all, a kind of game for sovereigns.

"Therefore, modern European scholars who advocate the abolition of war and the promotion of peace all insist on the merits of democracy. When democracy is achieved, they hope to unite all the nations of the world into a large federation. This dream might seem far-fetched, but from the point of view of the law of political evolution, it is not necessarily so unrealistic.

"O god of evolution! Turn your wheels more quickly and spur your horse. Nurture what is growing, cut down what is withering, and let millions of people on earth live a free and satisfying life! Ah, the several hundred million free people of Europe! In your respective countries, the civil law, the criminal law, and other laws protect you, your property, and your homes. You cannot be harmed at random. And even if some brutal person should injure you, the law will punish him immediately and you will be comforted. If someone destroys your property, you need not grapple with him. Simply bring suit with a single piece of paper. An impartial judge who decides the case according to clearly defined laws will give you compensation. You have indeed passed through the dangerous stage of savage conflict and entered the system of peace and civilization.

"Cast your eyes, citizens of Europe, beyond your national boundaries. The weapons which your neighbors manufacture are designed some day to kill you with one blast and to burn down your homes in a flash. The warships and torpedoes they build are meant to shake your houses and the trees along your beaches. Today you sleep peacefully, but tomorrow you may become corpses in the field. Individuals live a civilized life, and individual families also

86

live a civilized and peaceful life. But when people band together into larger political entities, they live a savage life.
Nations, which are groups of families, live under the constant threat of savagery.

"If smallpox spreads, it is possible to prevent the disease by vaccination. If malaria strikes, we can protect ourselves with carbolic acid. But we cannot protect ourselves
from our neighboring enemy's shells. We can compensate
for burned houses or capsized boats with insurance. But we
cannot stay the disaster of war waged by our neighbors. Do
you really fear that your enemy will some day kill or wound
you with a sword, burn your crops and buildings, or blow
up your harbors? Then why don't you quickly demolish
your guns? Why don't you burn your warships?

"Today, in the nineteenth century, it is indeed an insane
nation which takes pride in military power, makes aggression its national policy, and tries to own the earth, regardless of means, by usurping someone else's land or by killing
someone else's people. But there is in fact such an insane
country at the eastern edge of Europe. You can tell by
looking at the national policy which its sovereigns have
handed down to their posterity. Germany is shocked and
remorseful at her own use of such violent poison and the
unexpectedly devastating result. France is humiliated and
angry because her complacency led to her defeat. Great
Britain has purchased a large amount of land and amassed a
great fortune; she fears theft, and is deeply worried about
her protection. Italy is a child who doesn't realize that while
adults may live a life of excessive indulgence, they also have
many concerns on their mind; the child envies them greatly
and wants to join them. Belgium, Holland, and Switzerland
are like lovely little children who play, without getting
hurt, in the midst of four or five madmen who fight by
swinging sticks at each other. And the United States? She
watches the warriors of a certain feudal nation carry the

87

honor of their domains on their shoulders, competing in bravery and hatred.* She laughs at them and refuses to deal with them, concentrating her efforts on her family business and saving a great deal of wealth.

"A certain large Asian country has a dull mind and spirit and limbs that are heavy and clumsy, but it is not afraid of fighting because it relies on its large size. The islands of Asia are like children who have united because, physically weak and timid, they occasionally suffer torments inflicted by bullies from the outside. Haven't you noticed that there is a child prodigy among these islands? There is no way of predicting what this child will be like in future.

"What blind fools the Europeans are! France and Germany were at one point united under Charlemagne. Later, France under Louis XIV attacked and conquered Germany without provocation. Later still, Prussia under Frederick II defeated France and thus took its revenge. Then France under Napoleon Bonaparte again attacked and defeated Germany without provocation. More recently, Prussia under Kaiser Wilhelm defeated France and again took its revenge. If two nations continue to attack each other for revenge, generation after generation, where will the fighting end? Prussia under Kaiser Wilhelm and France under Napoleon III were locked into a grudge fight against each other. But what grudge can exist between the Prussian people and the French people?

"The Prussians as a people and the French as a people are civilized men of learning, not foolhardy warriors. France

* This is probably a reference to Spain. Between Napoleon's invasion of Spain in 1808 and the defeat of Spain in the Spanish-American War, the Spanish experienced a long succession of periods of domestic unrest, oscillating between absolute monarchy and anarchy, with conservative and progressive factions fighting for supremacy. To some extent, Japan's situation in the nineteenth century was similar.

88

has already become a France of the French people. When Prussia belongs to the Prussian people, the two nations will become united as brothers. The quickness of France and the calm of Prussia will be united in a bond of friendship.

"But Russia? The Russians *are* foolhardy warriors. Can you, Russia, cease as well to be the Russia of Czar Alexander and become a Russia of the Russian people? I know, of course, that this is the profound significance of the drastic methods frequently employed by the violent Anarchist faction.

"Now England, too, is a civilized country of learning that enjoys accumulating wealth. So if Great Britain should perhaps commit violence in Africa or Asia, the truth of the matter is that she fears Russian violence, and only acts as a last resort. . . . Great Britain, France, Russia, and Germany—please be careful not to produce a monster called 'champion' among your peoples. And if, by some misfortune, this monster should appear, don't listen to him. If you should make the mistake of listening to his words, you will no longer be your own masters, but will become his possessions.

"I want to say one more thing. Many large nations on earth are fools. They not only invite disaster upon themselves by adhering to monarchy, but they have brought, or are about to bring, disaster upon their sovereigns. Why don't small nations venture to adopt democracy and thereby make themselves and their sovereigns happy? Many of the strong nations on earth are cowards. Fearing each other, they maintain troops and line up battleships, and thus fall into danger. Why don't the weak nations voluntarily and firmly dismiss their soldiers, dissolve their fleets, and choose peace?"

The Champion drew closer and said, "What Mr. Gentle-

89

man has said is quite scholarly. A scholar's words can be written in a book but cannot be practiced. Mr. Gentleman, go to London, Paris, Berlin, or Saint Petersburg and express your learned opinions with all your might. The journalists of these countries may print your views on the 'miscellaneous' pages, partly for amusement, but the politicians would perhaps—"

"The politicians would surely consider me mad," interrupted the Gentleman of Western Learning. "But I would be most proud to be treated as mad by politicians! Oh, for some scholars! Today's so-called politicians are hopelessly inept at government. Scholars! We need scholars! As the ancients said, 'Unless a philosopher administers the affairs of state, real peace cannot be expected.' How true is the saying!"*

The Champion replied, "I understand, Mr. Gentleman. But I need to ask you one thing. You recommend that the weak and small nations immediately adopt democracy and abolish their armed forces. Behind your recommendation, isn't there a faint sense of expectation that powerful democratic nations such as the United States and France might be impressed with the greatness of the will and the excellence of the task and step in to help?"

The Gentleman was quick to respond. "Indeed not! Whenever one must make an important decision on national policy, relying on such mere chance is precisely the main cause for failure. I see only moral principles as having any importance. Whether or not the United States and France might be impressed with our strong will and lofty goals and offer us help, or whether or not Russia, Great Britain, and Germany might try to protect us because of their concern with the balance of power, that's their concern, not mine."

* Gentleman obviously refers here to Plato, whose theories regarding the philosopher-king are set forth in his *Republic*.

"Then what would you do," said the Champion, "if some vicious nation should take advantage of our disarmament and send its troops to attack us?"

The Gentleman answered, "I firmly believe that there is no such nation. If there were indeed such a vicious nation, we would have no choice but to find our own countermeasures. It is my hope that without calling up a single soldier or producing a single bullet, we would calmly state, 'We have never committed any incivility against you. We have no reason to be blamed. We have no internal disputes in the harmonious working of our government. We do not want you to disturb our country. Please go home immediately.' If the invaders would refuse to listen, loading their rifles and taking aim, we would simply cry in a loud voice, 'How uncivil and inhuman you are!' We would then be shot to death. I have no special remedy."

The Champion could not keep from laughing. "That philosophical ideas should blind the human mind to such an extent! Mr. Gentleman, you've spent several hours discussing the condition of the world and dissecting political history, but according to you, the last resort is for all citizens of the nation to clasp their hands in submission and fall victim to enemy bullets. What a simple-minded tale! Is this the divine power of the famous god of evolution? Fortunately, I'm certain that most people will never rely on the benevolence of such a god."

A great argument concerning the law of self-defense.

"Among European scholars," replied the Gentleman of Western Learning, "those who are against war maintain that aggression is immoral but defense is moral. Their view is an attempt to apply an individual's right of self-defense to political entities. But in my opinion, such thinking runs counter to the essential truth. Why? By nature, murder is evil; it destroys the order of life. Therefore, if someone wishes to kill you,

91

you should not kill him even if he is a thief or an outlaw. If you try to kill someone because he is trying to kill you, then it follows that because someone else intends evil, you should also do evil.

"Some may say, 'Life is most precious, yet this thief tried to take my life without any reason. I killed him to preserve my own precious life.' I answer that life is indeed precious. But if your life is precious, so is your adversary's, regardless of whether or not he is a thief. Thus it is better to concentrate on self-defense to preserve your life and wait for the arrival of police. If you go ahead and take the thief's life instead, you are acting against the wisdom of philosophy.

"In the meantime, the right of legitimate self-defense is a practical necessity for individuals. But if we try to apply this right to nations, a basic irrationality emerges. If, when an enemy attacks us, we summon our troops and protect ourselves with guns, our defensive act becomes an attack in itself and must be considered an evil deed. Therefore, to apply the individual's right of self-defense to entire nations is contrary to the deepest truths of philosophy. Mr. Champion, I would prefer that our people call up no soldiers and carry no bullets, but die at the hands of the invading enemy troops, because I wish to transform us into living embodiments of moral principles and to make us a model for future generations. Your theory states that because the other person does evil, I should also do evil. But isn't that the height of barbarity?'"

Master Nankai had been listening to this exchange without uttering a word, but at this point he took a drink and also offered cups to the two guests, saying, "I have listened to Mr. Gentleman's learned argument. Mr. Champion, please enlighten me with your excellent views."

The Champion began his response. "First, no matter how detestable it may be for scholars, war exists, and is an inevitable force in the actual world. Moreover, it is our

92

counter
argument
to the other
guy

nature as animals to love victory and hate defeat. Every living thing between heaven and earth, from the insects to such fierce beasts as tigers, lions, coyotes, and wolves, lives by catching and killing its prey. Observe the animals closely. Among living things, the wiser creatures are also the braver. The stupid creatures are more cowardly. Ducks are the silliest of the birds, and pigs the stupidest of the animals. Ducks cannot kick or bite, but can only quack. Pigs can neither kick nor bite, and can only squeal. Yet can we say that these two creatures are kind and humane?

"Or look at children. Just as soon as they can start crawling about, they will swing sticks to hit dogs or cats whenever they see them, or drag them by their tails, while their round, childish faces are all smiles and joy. Only children who are sick and listless do not do these things. Besides, indignation is an expression of moral sense. No one has moral sense without getting angry. A cat that catches a mouse acts under a cat's moral sense. A wolf that catches a deer follows a wolf's moral sense. Can we say that these two animals are inhumane? The expression 'These animals are inhumane' is blatant anthropomorphism.

unrestrained
paragraph

"Even scholars, who seem to value theories and despise conflict, in reality simply love to win and hate to lose. Look at them. When two scholars express their respective views face to face, they argue and refute each other until their voices grow harsh. Then they draw closer, their eyes flashing, flailing their arms and yelling at each other, no longer listening to each other's words. Their response is predictable: 'It's not that I want to win but that I want my principle to win.' But this is an empty excuse. If they really want their principles to win, why don't they express their views calmly and dispassionately?

"A quarrel results from the anger of individuals. War is the result of the anger of states. Those who refuse to quarrel are cowards. Those nations that refuse to fight wars are weak.

If anyone says that quarreling is a vice and war an absurdity, let me ask him to consider this: What can be done about the fact that individuals actually possess vices? What can be done about the fact that states act absurdly? In short, what can be done about reality?

"Therefore, civilized nations are always strong. They fight wars but do not have civil strife, for since they have strict laws, their citizens do not quarrel. It is because these nations maintain powerful military forces that they cannot avoid wars with other countries. Savage people never cease to quarrel. When would they have time left for war? If you investigate history, the civilized nations of antiquity were those that fought brilliantly. The civilized nations of today are those that now fight brilliantly. Sparta fought superbly. So did Rome. In modern times, Great Britain, France, Germany, and Russia are the most brilliant fighters. As society progresses and intellectual faculties develop, the number of soldiers increases, weapons improve, and fortresses become more secure. Therefore, armaments are a measure of the achievement of each nation. War is a thermometer that tests the strength of each nation's civilization. When two nations are about to engage in war, the one with superior learning and greater wealth will surely win, because it has superior weapons. Of the five continents, Europe has the most advanced civilization and the most superior armaments, so it is the strongest in war. We have such clear-cut evidence. Who can dispute it?

"Russia, with over a million soldiers, is about to swallow Turkey and Korea. Germany, too, with its million-plus soldiers, has crushed France and is now ready to expand into Asia. France, with a comparable army, now tries to take revenge on Germany, and has recently invaded the territory of Annam. And Great Britain, with its fleet of over a hundred battleships, has colonies all over the world. Can't you see what the strong European nations have been doing

94

recently? With glaring eyes, Russia, Great Britain, Germany, and France are rolling up their sleeves, ready to move at the first chance. The situation is as dangerous as a pile of explosives rolling about on the ground. Once they explode, millions of soldiers will trample the fields of Europe and thousands of battleships will invade the seas of Asia. To insist narrow-mindedly on the ideals of liberty and equality, or to express the sentiment of universal brotherhood at such a time is like Lu Xiufu's insistence on teaching the classics as the Mongol armies attacked, isn't it?*

"The sizzling heat of summer can make a person feel as if he is being steamed or scorched. Yet imagine someone sitting, European-style, on a chair at a desk on a hot day. He opens his book and mutters something, or closes his eyes and meditates. His face is covered with streams of perspiration and his back is soaked with sweat, but he does not feel the heat. Or imagine this same scholar on a winter night, about four o'clock in the morning, when the candlelight grows faint. The fireplace is cold, and the water in the inkstone freezes even before he mixes enough ink to write with. There is no warmth in any part of his body—hands, feet, head, face, chest, stomach, or back. Still he remains at the desk. Still he opens his book and mutters something or closes his eyes and meditates. He simply does not feel the cold.

"What pleasure can he have? —Do not be fooled: he has intense pleasure. The wisdom in his brain has become the supreme commander of all the power of his heart. With

---

* When the Song dynasty (960–1279) was about to fall at the hands of Mongol invaders, Prime Minister Lu Xiufu continued to lecture the eight-year-old emperor on the *Great Learning* (*Da Xue*). The Song dynasty finally collapsed when the prime minister was forced to commit suicide by drowning with the young sovereign on his back. Chōmin uses this episode as an example of useless idealism, though he cites the *Analects* (*Lun Yu*) instead of the *Great Learning*. See Kuwabara and Shimada, p. 234.

inductive logic as his guns and rifles and deductive logic as his battleships, he is trying to destroy error—a strong enemy indeed—and to enter the city of truth.

"This feeling of triumph is a very great pleasure that we have all felt. For merchants, the pleasure lies in defeating a mighty enemy called stagnating market conditions and in amassing a large profit. For farmers, the pleasure lies in defeating a mighty enemy called unseasonable weather and in reaping a good harvest. In every field, everyone, whatever their job or skill, seeks a triumph. There is no one who does not desire this pleasure. Every individual has pleasures of his own; can a nation do without them? What gives an individual pleasure is his own satisfaction. What gives a nation this pleasure is the wisdom of the premier's policy and the general's strategy. If our policy is excellent, other nations will rush to make treaties with us. If our strategy is superb, the enemy will be defeated after a single battle. How exhilarating is the pleasure of a nation!

"Mr. Gentleman is obsessed with the idea that war is undesirable. He pictures the suffering of soldiers exposed to wind and rain and believes that it is real. He imagines the pain of soldiers being scorched and thinks that it is real. But is the suffering real? Is the pain real? War requires courage, and courage requires spirit. When a battle is about to start, men become almost mad, and their courage begins to boil over. They are in a new and completely different world. Where is there any place for pain? Suppose the enemy is camped at a certain location only a few miles away from our forces. Our commander has sent scouts to pinpoint the enemy situation. Our troops will go the long way around that mountainside or take this secret path; they will reach behind the enemy or appear at the enemy's flank. Taking the enemy by surprise, they will then fire cannon and rifles simultaneously, make an assault under the cover

96

of gunsmoke, and charge with the wind behind them. In this way, we will certainly win at one stroke.

"I will leap out to take the lead. If I survive, I will become the most courageous man in our army. If I die, my name will go down in history. This is the pleasure of a soldier, and a great pleasure it is. But Mr. Gentleman is fearless in his own way, too. He is not afraid of severe cold or extreme heat, and will continue to open his book and mutter something or close his eyes and meditate in spite of them. He will not feel the pain. How then could a military man consider death and injury as pain?

"Imagine a vast plain with no houses within twenty-five miles. Surrounding the plain are undulating hills like a long row of folding screens. The sky is clear and the wind calm; the morning sun shines on the frost. The field is covered with withered grass that breaks if one steps on a thin stem. It is late autumn or early winter. The enemy forces occupy a position in front of us. Their number may be a hundred thousand, or a hundred and ten thousand, or even a hundred and twenty thousand. Their leader is Commander So-and-so, famed as a skilled strategist. Their soldiers are strong and their weapons are effective. We have a hundred thousand soldiers, all brave and dauntless, who believe passionately in my command. If we win, we shall pursue our enemy without giving him a chance to breathe. We will penetrate into his capital city, force him to yield his land, and demand reparation. If peace is made, our kingdom's military authority will shine in all four directions. If we don't win, we will die and leave our brave legacy behind us in the world. This challenge is the pleasure of a commander. And it is a very great pleasure indeed. Mr. Gentleman, you may choose writing as your pleasure; let me choose war as mine."

When Master Nankai heard these words, he smiled and

97

said, "You are both young and vigorous. You may well pursue your own pleasures. But herein lies my only pleasure." So saying, he emptied one or two drinks, rubbed his chest, and sighed, "Ah, what fun!"

The Gentleman of Western Learning said, "Mr. Champion, you and I are discussing the nation's policy, not personal pleasures. You seem to have digressed a bit."

Master Nankai offered some defense of the Champion. "Mr. Champion has aptly explored the inner workings of human nature and has described human pleasures well. He seems to have learned from psychologists' studies."

But the Champion answered, "I have made a mistake. Forgive me. I will proceed directly to the main issue.

"Today all the nations of the world are competing to promote military strength. All the wonderful discoveries and results of scientific learning are utilized for war, and military technology becomes ever more advanced. In other words, physics, chemistry, and mathematics make guns superior and fortresses more secure; agriculture, industry, and commerce also supply the expenses for weapons or provisions for the military. In effect, all enterprises flow into one place, and all activities support military policies. This is why a million soldiers and a fleet of several hundred or several thousand battleships can proceed immediately toward the enemy stronghold or run toward the enemy port the minute the order is given, without delay or disobedience.

"Indeed, for those who must govern their nation under the eyes of countless tigers and wolves, on what else but military preparations can they rely to protect their land?

"And yet, our opponent may have a million troops to our hundred thousand. He may have a hundred or even a thousand battleships, while we have no more than a few dozen. If such is the case, no matter how hard we may train ourselves to reach peak efficiency, our strength will still be that of a child. It will amount to nothing but an amusing and fleeting show. To try to protect ourselves from foreign nations with our scant forces is either stupidity or insanity. It is sheer luck that our harbors have not yet been blown up. It is mere chance that our fortresses have not been burned down. Our opponents have never feared us. They simply have their own reasons why they cannot invade us yet. But once they decide to invade us, they will do so immediately. Our harbors will indeed be blown up, our fortresses burned down, our countryside torn to pieces, and our capital city . . . Ah, in today's world, what a precarious existence we small nations have!

"Even so, it is impossible to make our small land instantly large, our poor nation suddenly rich, and to increase immediately the size of our army or enlarge our fleet. But unless we build up the number of soldiers and battleships and increase our nation's wealth and enlarge our land, we may perish. *This* is the simple logic of arithmetic. Haven't you learned from the examples of Poland and Burma?* Fortunately, we now have the means to enlarge and enrich our nation and to increase our troops and battleships. Why don't we start immediately?

Mr. Champion is slightly behind the times.

"I seem to have forgotten whether it is in Asia or in Africa, but there is a large country. I've forgotten its name, but it is vast and rich in natural resources. In some ways, however, it is very weak. I hear that this

---

* Poland's subjugation to foreign powers had a long history even before the First Partition of 1772 by Russia, Austria, and Prussia. Subsequent partitions and agreements reached at the Congress of Vienna (1814–15) intensified the repression of the Polish people.

After a series of Anglo-Burmese Wars, the British annexed the entire kingdom of Burma in 1886. Although the Burmese continued to resist, the British army finally prevailed by 1890 and the colonization of Burma was complete.

country has over a million soldiers, but they are confused and undisciplined, and will be useless in an emergency. I also hear that the government of this nation is as good as nothing—a big, fat sacrificial cow. This is what heaven provides as nourishment for small nations like us to fill our bellies with. Why shouldn't we go and tear off a half or a third of that country? If we issue an imperial decree summoning all the able-bodied men of our nation, we should be able to gather at least four or five hundred thousand men. If we are willing to give up our nation's savings, we should be able to buy at least several dozen to several hundred battleships. If we send soldiers to fight, merchants to trade, farmers to cultivate, artisans to manufacture, and scholars to teach, and if we take a half or a third of that country and make it part of ours, our nation will suddenly become large. Since we will then have, under our enlightened government, an abundance of materials and a large population, we will be able to build fortresses, manufacture guns, mobilize a million strong soldiers on land, and maintain a hundred or a thousand battleships on the sea. Our small nation will instantly change into a Russia or a Great Britain.

"What shall we do with our small original land? Since we have already obtained a new and larger land, we no longer need to be concerned with our original plot. Our emperor, accompanied by Admiral So-and-so, General X, Lieutenant General Y, and Major General Z as his guards, will himself lead the main troops and cross the sea on our invincible man-of-war X. Taking advantage of the fact that battalion X won a great victory earlier, our emperor chooses a certain location as his new capital and builds his new palace. Its architecture is truly magnificent. Its many-storied tower rises above the clouds; the imperial guards take their position in a circle; the imperial guard cavalry are stationed all around. It is unmistakably the residence of an emperor.

"Our emperor is now the emperor of our new, expanded country. As for our small original country, we will let a foreign country take it if anyone cares to. If Russia comes first, we will give it to Russia. If Great Britain comes first, we will give it to Great Britain. But no. That is not good policy. On our original plot of land, we have advocates of civil rights and democracy, many of whom do not like the sovereign or the military. Since our sovereign and our armed forces have moved to our big new country, let's give our original country to these disciples of civil rights and democracy. They wil greatly rejoice, will they not?

"What shall we do with the emperors' tombs? No matter how stubborn and radical they may be, and no matter how much they may hate the monarchy, the advocates of civil rights would never loathe the deceased sovereigns to the point of defiling their tombs. If we send an imperial messenger to offer a tribute every year, we will not be remiss in our observance of the ancestral rites.

"Now we have a large country, spacious territory, a large population, strong soldiers, and indestructible battleships. We promote agriculture, encourage commerce, subsidize industry, and enforce excellent policies. As our government increases its wealth, we will purchase the fruits of European and American civilization. The personal wealth of our people will also increase, and they will share in these fruits. How could Great Britain, France, Russia, and Germany scorn us then, no matter how haughty they may be?

"The strength and wealth of Great Britain, France, Germany, and Russia did not blossom overnight. Extremely complex causes and means were involved. Sometimes a philosopher-king administered a benevolent government; sometimes a prime minister of extraordinary character helped the sovereign and managed domestic affairs and foreign policies; a skilled general achieved military feats;

a great scholar advocated a profound theory; or a master craftsman created a finely wrought object. In times of peace those nations practiced accumulating wealth, and in times of war they endured hardships. Sometimes the rain moistened the earth, and sometimes the shining sun bleached it. At times their steep, narrow path opened out onto a flat plain; sometimes they left a rapid stream and entered a gentle river. They turned to the right or the left, gently or abruptly. After tens of thousands of injuries and sufferings, they finally entered the realm of modern civilization. But how many months and years, how much knowledge, how much labor, how many lives, and how much property have they expended?

"If we wish to rush into the realm of civilization and try to partake of its fruits, we have no other way but to purchase what we need by paying money. But the price of civilization is very high, and such advancements cannot be bought for a small amount. Therefore, if a small nation tries to buy them in a hurry, the nation's financial resources will be drained in an instant. If we try to pay for it a little at a time and buy it piece by piece, we will be swallowed up by one of the civilized nations before we have bought even a small portion. Even though we are small, the large nation can only gain, increasing its power and wealth, by swallowing us. And even if the large nation is humane and decides out of pity not to swallow us up, it is still a large, strong country, while ours is still small and weak. We will inevitably melt away of our own accord and evaporate like a drop of water exposed to direct sunlight. The sun may not mean to dry up the water, but the water will naturally evaporate. Such are the relationships between the strong and the weak, between the large and the small.

Some practical economic policy must surely originate from here some day.

102

"Therefore, any nation which lags behind in ob[...] the substance of civilization would, in effect, have to [...] it with a great deal of money—though the exact methods may vary. And since a small nation cannot afford to finance that cost, it must seize a big country by force and make itself rich. Fortunately, by the grace of heaven, right in front of us is a large country whose soil is fertile and whose soldiers are weak. Could we possibly have better luck? If this large country were strong, it would be impossible for us to take it by force and obtain its wealth, even if we wanted to. But fortunately this large country is lazy and easy to deal with. Why shouldn't a small nation quickly seize it? Isn't it infinitely better to seize it and enrich and strengthen ourselves than not to seize it and face annihilation?"

Mr. Champion took another drink and continued. "Even if we concentrate on improving domestic affairs in order to pave the way to becoming a civilized nation some day, the necessity of invading a foreign country is unavoidable under present circumstances. I'll explain why.

"Any nation deciding to climb the path of civilization behind other nations must completely change its earlier culture, character, customs, and feelings. It is thus natural that two opposing groups will emerge within its population: the lovers of nostalgia and the lovers of novelty. For the nostalgic, all the new culture, character, customs, and feelings seem shallow and exaggerated. They think that their eyes are soiled by looking at the new things and their ears dirtied with the new sounds. They feel dizzy and nauseated by any mention of the new.

"The lovers of novelty are just the opposite. For them, everything old seems spoiled and fetid. Afraid of being left behind, they become engrossed in the pursuit of the new. Even those who do not obviously belong to these two extremes will, upon closer scrutiny, necessarily drift toward

103

group. The preservers of the old and the
~~~~~ are two incompatible elements, like ice

~~~~~ to analyze these two elements, but we can
~~~~~guish them by their ages and certain regional
~~~~~ Try to examine actual cases. People over
~~~~~erally nostalgic and those under thirty are
usually novelty seekers. In other words, closer observation
reveals that even those over thirty who willingly try to
adopt new things and who seem genuinely to like them
are ruled by nostalgia, which arises without their knowledge
and exerts its force on them almost constantly. As for those
under thirty, their education, under their fathers' influence,
may inevitably be tinged with nostalgia, but their sponta-
neous acts naturally express a love of novelty that is incompatible with the nostalgic urge. This is no surprise. When
those over thirty were twelve or thirteen, when they began
to understand life, their daily chores included reciting the
Book of Songs and *Book of Documents,* reading the *Analects* and
*Mencius,** or practicing swordsmanship or spear handling.
Everything they saw, heard, or took an interest in was part of
the old culture, and such things became deeply engraved
in their minds and could not be erased. Those under thirty
were steeped in new things before any of the older images
were impressed on their minds, and the love of the new
easily dominated their thinking. This is why these two
generations differ so greatly.

"Some may say that many of those over thirty began to
study books written in English or French in their youth,
or read various books in translation, or were active in the
progressive movements of their time and learned the

* The *Book of Songs* (*Shi Jing*), *Book of Documents* (*Shu Jing*), *Analects* (*Lun
Yu*), and *Mencius* (*Mengzi*) are all part of the Confucian canon.

104

concepts of freedom, equality, rights, and responsibility. Not to be outdone by the younger generations, they have made, some say, efforts to enter the path of the new, and therefore one cannot distinguish the two groups by age. Such a contention seems quite reasonable. People gifted with special insight and knowledge cannot, of course, be discussed in terms of ordinary logic. But the exception proves the rule. Only a tiny minority are free from the conditioning of their age.

Does a man with a gift of true perceptiveness and extraordinary knowledge really exist in this world? —Yes, he does.

"As an experiment, observe any man over thirty who lives with his wife and child. If he sees his child use a silk parasol to keep off the summer sun or wear a woolen shawl to keep out the winter cold, he will scold the child by saying, 'What a weakling you are! Why shun the scorching sun? Why fear the cold wind?' It's not that he wants his child to become hardened to the effects of cold and heat. He objects simply because he never used a parasol or a shawl when he was a child. If he hears his wife discuss learning, art, or current affairs, he severely reprimands her, saying, 'You're a woman. All you need to worry about is the kitchen. Don't talk about these matters again, or you'll be laughed at.' Again, it's not because he is afraid of becoming a henpecked husband, but because in his youth he never heard women talk about these things. But behind his back his child will say, 'How ignorant of the rules of health my barbarian father is.' And his wife will say in his absence, 'My stubborn husband is so far behind the times.' This case suggests why the two elements, the nostalgic and the lovers of the new, can be classified according to age.

"These two elements can also be distinguished according to regional characteristics. During the feudal period, for

example, large *han* with over two hundred thousand *koku**
usually closed their boundaries to people from other domains. Throughout their lives the inhabitants saw and heard
only what took place within their own domain, and the only
people they came into contact with were the people of their
domain. Consequently, a certain fixed pattern emerged
in their thought, customs, clothing, and even language, and
a distinct cultural unit was formed. In small domains with
less than two hundred thousand *koku*, the same thing
happened in remote towns and villages, which also had no
contact with other domains. The customs of these domains
are simple and honest and the citizens value military power,
a common trait in such regions. Most of them are generous
and sincere, rustic but manly, though some are jealous and
tricky, slow and stupid. Most of these people still yearn
for the past and dislike the new. They are given to resentment and righteous indignation, but are not meticulous or
refined.

"In domains located where traffic was open in all directions, the inhabitants constantly came into contact with
things and people from different regions. They lived excit-
ing if somewhat confused lives. Consequently, their customs were elaborate, they valued literature rather than
military power, and the people there grew quick and sophisticated. On the negative side, they tended to be sycophantic and shallow. At any rate, many were quick to abandon
the old and adopt the new. Again, those with exceptional
learning and special insight cannot be discussed in terms of
ordinary logic, but as I said before, only a few people are
free from the influence of regional characteristics. For this

* A *han* was the fief of a daimyo, or feudal lord, in the Edo period (1603–
1868). The size of a *han* was represented by the number of *koku*—a measure of rice—its daimyo received as a stipend from the central government. One *koku* was equal to approximately four bushels.

reason, I maintain that the lovers of nostalgia and lovers of the new can usually be classified according to regional characteristics. ⇒ there are vesicles

"In a nation which has begun to climb the path of civilization late and only now faces the opportunity for reform, these two elements permeate the society, both in the government as well as outside it. These two trends sneak into the hearts of all the citizens of the nation, officials as well as the common people, and vie with each other everywhere in a constant struggle for victory. The battle between the old and the new divides the premier and the other ministers. The same forces cause divisions among government officials, civilians, farmers, artisans, and merchants. They create rifts between parents and children, between husbands and wives, among young people, and among friends. From the grand hundred-year plans issued by the imperial court to the day-to-day work of the people, from explicit face-to-face debates to more trivial matters such as food and personal taste, wherever human judgment is involved, these two elements always repel and fight against each other, and are never harmonized. Thus, in any nation, the usual divisions of government and people, officials and civilians, and groups such as scholars, artists, farmers, artisans, and merchants are augmented by these two new and significant factions. This is a serious disease, and very hard to cure.

"Suppose, for example, that Minister or General X comes from former domain A. Minister or General Y comes from former domain B. Domain A was large, or perhaps located in an out-of-the-way place, with no contact with other domains. Its customs were simple and honest, and military power was valued. Many of its people were large-hearted and sincere, though some were jealous and shiftless. Domain B was small, or perhaps located in the area where traffic was open in all directions. As I've said, its customs were refined and literature was highly valued. Its people were quick and sophisticated, though some were sycophantic and shallow. From this information, I can see clearly which former domain is influenced more by nostalgia and which by novelty. This is not, of course, an iron-clad rule, and it is impossible to generalize about special men with extraordinary perceptiveness and knowledge.

"Minister or General X is between forty and fifty years of age, while Minister or General Y is between twenty and thirty. From this alone, I can clearly see which official is more influenced by nostalgia and which is more influenced by novelty—though, as I have said, in the case of a man of extraordinary insight and knowledge this is impossible to determine.

"Among ordinary citizens, even those who advocate the principle of liberty and who agree on the need for reform, nostalgia and novelty exert their invisible power and leave their stamp. Those more inclined to novelty, for example, value theories, despise physical force, and give priority to developing industry instead of weapons. They study the theoretical

*Members of the former Liberal and Progressive parties.**

bases of moral principles and the law, examine the laws of economics, always take pride in being literati or scholars, and reject soldiers and champions and their bold manner of righteous indignation. They admire Thiers and Gladstone, but not Napoleon or Bismarck.

"Those more inclined to nostalgia are quite different. They regard freedom as willful and irresponsible behavior

* The Liberal Party (Jiyūtō), established in 1881 and dissolved in 1884, was the political party which served as the core of the popular rights movement. "Progressives" (Kaishintō) is an abbreviation for the Constitutional Reform Progressive Party (Rikken Kashintō). Established in 1882 and dissolved in 1896, this political party advocated constitutional monarchy modeled after that of Great Britain.

and equality as an axe that destroys by leveling all. They take pleasure in giving vent to resentment and righteous indignation, and dislike stifling jurisprudence or complicated economics.

"When these lovers of nostalgia read the history of the French Revolution, they pay no attention to the fact that in the midst of a great upheaval from top to bottom, the Legislative Assembly and the People's Assembly established an immortal system that raised the curtain for the new world of the nineteenth century. But when they learn that Robespierre, Danton, and others committed brutal murders at will, they jump up and cry, 'Delightful!' With watering mouths, they wish they could do what these Frenchmen did. This should come as no surprise. Until about twenty or thirty years ago, these men regarded swinging swords, wielding spears, and dying in battle as the incomparable honor. Their reverence for military power was inherited from their remote ancestors. The three-foot-long swords of the ancestors were their symbols for it. These swords, which had been handed down from generation to generation, were treasured until the decree abolishing the wearing of swords was issued.* In tears they packed away their swords in chests, but there is not one among them who does not privately wish to have a chance to take out his sword and use it.

The former Liberals will surely object and jeer.

"Later, when the ideas of liberty and democracy arrived from abroad, these men became engulfed in them. They formed associations and gathered everywhere, displaying their party flags. Those who were warriors until only recently have now instantly become dignified politicians of the civilized world. But are they truly the politicians of

* In 1876.

109

civilization? They had originally cherished the ideal of dying in battle, but they found no outlet for it and became frustrated. When by chance they learned of democracy and liberty, they found in them something decisive and vehement, and joyfully thought, 'These ideas resemble our ideal of dying in battle. We must exchange our ideal of dying in battle, which is a relic of the feudal system, for this democracy imported from foreign lands.'

"I have just explained the evolution of these men's thinking. But their progress is not true progress. These men are very fond of a parliament because it is a convenient place to yell loudly, or to oppose the premier and other ministers. These men are quite fond of revolution, but their 'revolution' is not a case of discarding the old and adopting the new. Rather, they simply like change, be it for better or for worse. They are drawn to destruction because it superficially resembles bravery. Similarly, they dislike constructiveness because it seems to resemble cowardice. They hate preservation the most, because it seems most closely to resemble cowardice.

"When these men find that they cannot become members of Parliament because they are ineligible to run, they establish their headquarters in a half-ruined temple in a certain ward in the southern part of the capital, or perhaps in the northern part of the capital, where they devote all their strength to attacking ministers, members of Parliament, and journalists.*

"They like to attack, but they don't know why they attack. After a while they publish a newspaper. Which words

* In an 1891 editorial for *Rikken Jiyū Shimbun* (Constitutional Liberty Newspaper) Chōmin urges the voters to establish "clubs" ("headquarters" in the present paragraph) and meeting places as well as to join political parties. The "newspaper" in the next paragraph most likely refers to *Jiyū Shimbun* (Liberty Newspaper), the official newspaper of the Jiyūtō party. Chōmin was on its editorial staff from June to October 1882.

appear most frequently in its editorial columns? I know that 'overthrow,' 'destruction,' 'slaughter,' and 'carnage' appear with more than a little frequency. They use expressions such as 'ripping open the guts and heads,' 'spilling lifeblood,' and 'decapitation' to make their writing more dramatic. It has just occurred to me that the Frenchmen Marat and Saint-Just must have belonged to the nostalgic element three or four years before the French Revolution.

"When the two elements of nostalgia and novelty oppose each other head-on at the imperial court, how much hindrance it causes to national policy making! History shows how often such a phenomenon can cause a headache and a frown.

The line-up of political wrestlers.

"Lovers of nostalgia have stern looks and possess—or at least seem to—a heroic spirit. If an emergency arises, they always act resolutely, heedless of repercussions or public opinion. In times of peace, they are content to remain calm and idle and to keep their mouths shut, disdaining any involvement in matters which require meticulous thinking and smooth execution since they regard them as trivial. They say: 'I was born incompetent; I have no ability for this. So-and-so is clever, talented, and enthusiastic in his work. He is the one to deal with this matter.' In other words, in ordinary times and when dealing with ordinary matters, they believe it wise to play the fool, to play inept, to plead ignorance even when they are knowledgeable, to plead incompetence even when they are competent, and thereby let someone else do the job for them. In short, they believe that these matters are too trivial for their lofty minds. But if the problem is potentially serious, these men will raise their heads and express their views. And no matter how heated other people's arguments may become, these men show no concern. Disregarding what anyone else says, they aim at putting their own words into practice. They consider it the worst shame to change course and follow someone else's conviction.

"Lovers of novelty are different. Whenever something happens, whether it is significant or not, they always take a cautious attitude, racking their brains to ponder and examine the entire matter meticulously. Until it becomes clear to them that there will be no ill effect whatever, they will not take decisive action. Therefore, they usually have alert looks and their attitudes are, or seem to be, calm and sincere.

"Those who are nostalgic try not to bend; those who seek novelty aim not to fail. Today as always, when these two factions coexist in the government, its policy often becomes incomprehensible. There is no mystery in this. When these two forces fight head-on and the nostalgic element wins, government policy will reflect determination. If the element of novelty wins, the government will reflect caution. If you review the government decrees given over a period of several years, or in some extreme cases, over a period of several months, you'll find that the direction of these policies shifts considerably depending upon which force dominates.

"The differences in the personalities of the officials selected by either side are even greater. Each side naturally recommends those with whom it is pleased and selects those whom it loves. Thus, the lovers of novelty eagerly reach out for those officials who are talented, or seem so, and the lovers of nostalgia enthusiastically embrace those officials who have, or seem to have, integrity. This is, of course, the law of "psychological chemistry." The chiefs of many bureaus and departments as well as petty officials are drawn either by the nostalgic element or by the element of novelty. These officials attach

Civil servants all over the world are like this.

112

themselves to one of the two elements, become its henchmen, keep up appearances, and promote themselves so as to prepare for future benefits. History offers many examples of prestigious government offices being reduced to the haunts of these two factions.

"I ask you, Mr. Gentleman, wouldn't it be dangerous for any country where these two elements are competing with each other both within and outside of the government and struggling for victory, to have them some day clash head-on and fight to the finish? Even if that does not occur, and the two elements cautiously try to cooperate with each other, there is no telling how often the conflict between the two will recur since they are by nature incompatible. Unless we remove one of these two elements, it will become impossible to conduct national affairs, and I'm afraid that the god of evolution whom you worship will have no power at all."

The Gentleman asked, "If we must remove one of the two, which one should we eliminate?"

The Champion replied, "The nostalgic element. The element of novelty is like living flesh, and the nostalgic element is like a cancer." → dying

The Gentleman said, "Earlier you derided what I said, calling it a scholar's meaningless argument. But now, when you talk about the two elements existing in a nation which faces the opportunity to reform, you wish to retain the novelty seekers' element and to remove the nostalgic element, and you even go so far as to call the latter a cancer. Your argument seems contradictory, which goes to show that truth cannot be distorted."

The Champion laughed and said, "I see that you're a true believer in the element of novelty. You wish to adopt democracy and abolish the armed forces. I belong, of course, to the nostalgic element. I wish to save the country by

(cancer side)

113

military power. You know only how to fatten living flesh. I seek to remove the cancer for the good of the nation. Unless we remove the cancer, we cannot fatten the healthy flesh even if we want to.''

At this point the Gentleman asked, ''How would you remove this cancer?''

The Champion said, ''I'd simply cut it out ''

The appearance of a political surgeon.

The Gentleman grew impatient. ''Don't talk nonsense. A cancer is a diseased part of the body and can therefore be cut out. But the nostalgic element pervades the entire body. How can it be cut out? Please stop joking.''

The Champion replied, ''A cancer is to be cut out; the nostalgic element is to be killed.''

''And how,'' asked the Gentleman, ''can the nostalgic element be killed?''

The Champion said, ''We should drive them to war. Those of the nostalgic element, whether you find them at the imperial palace or at private homes in the town, all dislike peace and find safety painful. They feel helpless as they grow fat. If the state issues an order and starts a war, two or three hundred thousand men will gather instantly under the military banner. A person like me is a kind of cancer within society. I pray that I may cut myself out so as not to harm the living flesh of the nation forever. And there's no better place to remove the cancer than to that large country in Africa or Asia whose name I've forgotten. Therefore, I, together with two or three hundred thousand fellow 'cancer patients,' will go to that country. If we're successful, we will usurp the land, take firm root there, and establish what may be called a 'cancer society.' If we don't succeed, we will expose our dead bodies on the battlefield and leave our names in a foreign land. But whether we

114

succeed or not, we will have achieved the goal of removing the cancer for the good of the nation. This policy would kill two birds with one stone.

"Therefore, my first proposal is to gather all the able-bodied men of the land and move into that big country. By seizing it, we would change our nation from small to large, from weak to strong, and from poor to rich. Then we'll pay a huge sum of money to buy the fruits of civilization, and with one bound will attempt to compete with the European nations. The second proposal is to put our domestic affairs in order, reform our system of government, rectify public morals, and, in order to prepare our nation to become civilized in the future, remove once and for all the nostalgic faction, who will hinder our plans for reform. Those who are content with conventions, adhering to institutions designed to be only temporary measures; those who fear all decisive actions and consider it the best policy to float irresolutely—those people will be astounded beyond description when they learn of these two proposals. I fully realize that. But in all eras of history, champions who faced extraordinary challenges were able to devise extraordinary counterplans and achieve great results. As the saying goes, 'Firm resolution drives even a demon away.'

"It must also be remembered that politicians always adapt their methods to differing times and places. It would be total insanity to try to put my two proposals into practice in Europe today. Prussia, with Bismarck as prime minister and Moltke as general, mobilized a million soldiers, carried a million guns, and defeated France, against whom Prussia had sworn revenge for several hundred years with sustained determination and perseverance. But when peace was made, Prussia got only two states, Alsace and Lorraine, and eight hundred million francs—a settlement determined by the conditions of time and place. It would,

115

however, exactly fit the requirements of the times to put into practice my two proposals in Asia or Africa today. If you were to place an outstanding European leader in Asia today, I believe that he would without hesitation adopt one or the other of my two proposals. He'd either carry out the task of making the weak strong, or execute the plan to remove the cancer.''

"I see," said the Gentleman. "Napoleon and Tamerlane can be said to have adopted your two proposals. But it is precisely monsters such as these that greatly hinder the progress of society. These are the monsters that destroy the great ideals of liberty and equality as well as the harmonious workings of morality and economics. Instead they try to build a society based on physical force. If such brutes had not been born in the mountains of Europe since the eighteenth century, there is no question that democracy would have greatly expanded its supremacy and scholarly institutions would have enlarged their scope considerably.

"Compare European champions with our Oriental ones," the Gentleman continued. "In the Orient we have some so-called champions whom I consider to be monsters. But we have very few true champions in the Orient. Here is a point where the Orient is inferior to Europe. For example, Alexander, Caesar, and Napoleon may be compared with Liu Bang, Kublai Khan, and Toyotomi Hideyoshi.* But does the Orient offer any champions like Newton, Lavoisier, Adam Smith, and Auguste Comte? Clearly, those champions who devise temporary and violent policies to deal with immediate situations harm the great plans of the nation for the next hundred years."

* Liu Bang (248–195 B.C.) was the first Han emperor, also known as Gaozu. Kublai Khan (1216–94) was the grandson of Genghis Khan, founder of the Mongol dynasty and conqueror of China. Toyotomi Hideyoshi (1536–98) was a famous warrior general credited with the unification of Japan.

The Champion replied, "In every realm, a distinction exists between theory and practice. Theory wields power in debate, but practice achieves results in the real world. In medicine, we have medical theory and medical practice; in politics, political theory and political practice. Explanations of the workings of cells and viruses are medical theories. To administer quinine for a febrile disease or to use mercury for syphilis is medical practice. The principles of equality and economics are political theories. But to make the weak strong and to change disorder into order are political practice. You deal with the theory, Mr. Gentleman, and I'll discuss practice.

"Besides, if you look at the situation of Europe today, you'll see that those of us who try to survive on the Asian islands are like a lamp sputtering in a strong wind; if the wind gusts suddenly, the light goes out at once. Those concerned with the welfare of our country must take action soon, and my proposal to invade a foreign country fits the requirements of our times very well. As the children's saying goes, 'When the cat's away, the mice will play.' Now the cat is away. And who is the cat? None other than Germany, France, Russia, and Great Britain.

"Domestic and foreign newspapers alike are reporting in great detail the current situation in Germany and France. Some say that both countries are making efforts to prepare for war. Some say that there is hope of maintaining peace. Some report Bismarck's words and some report Boulanger's deeds. But as I have already revealed by examining the origin of the two nations' hostility, the explosion will happen soon—if not today, then tomorrow, and if not this year, then surely the next. Contrary to what Mr. Gentleman has said, it is not merely that the France of Emperor Napoleon III and the Prussia of Kaiser Wilhelm have formed a pact of hostility. Among the hostilities between nations in history none has been more intense than that between these two countries. Clearly, the cause did not develop in a single day. Napoleon and Wilhelm happened to be in power when the rupture took place. It was Bismarck's good fortune to be present at the time of the rupture and to exercise his political ability to the fullest. Gambetta, on the other hand, was not so fortunate. Lacking such an opportunity, he was unable to demonstrate his dauntless strategy. In his last years, Napoleon III gradually disappointed his people's expectations, and many within Parliament opposed him. However, when war was declared against Prussia, the members of Parliament all assented. Even though the veteran Thiers tried desperately to emphasize the disadvantage of war, Parliament loudly disagreed with him. It is said that on his way home from the sessions, a villainous mob ambushed him, jeering and throwing stones, which shows the extent of French hatred toward Prussia.

"However, according to my observations, France and Prussia did not originally have very deep hostilities toward each other. Since about the eighteenth century, however, these two countries have always been considered to have the strongest armies. Every time they fought each other, their neighboring countries would look on, excitedly predicting the winner and the loser. Consequently, the citizens of both countries have been pressured into a struggle for domination. They compete for power, feel ashamed of their previous defeats, and hold grudges against each other with a never-ending desire for revenge. They are like two sumō wrestlers in the ring. At first they intended only to compare their skills in a particular match. But the spectators raised their voices, praised the east side, lauded the west, and gave their thunderous applause when the game was over. When this was repeated several times, both wrestlers came to regard winning as a sacred duty and to harbor resentment

118

toward each other. The situation of France and Prussia is exactly the same. The two nations did not come to hate each other in a single day. Contrary to what the Gentleman has said, Kaiser Wilhelm's Prussia and Emperor Napoleon's France did not simply and immediately form a pact of mutual hostility.

"Now with Russia and Great Britain, however, the Gentleman's remarks are closer to the truth. Great Britain began early to pay special attention to its economy and developed colonies all over the earth. Consequently, no other nation can hope to match Great Britain's wealth. Her current purpose is to preserve her acquired territories. Expanding much further is not necessarily her goal. But Russia, like a fierce eagle, firmly adheres to the national policy handed down by her successive czars and tries to expand her territories vigorously. She relies on her military power, and, jealous of Great Britain's wealth and power, is obsessed with overthrowing India, which is England's colonial stronghold. This is why Great Britain recently allied with Napoleon III and fought at Sevastopol.

"The intention of France and Prussia is to compete with each other for military power or fame, but they do not wish to expand their territories. Great Britain concentrates on preserving its territories and wealth, and does not wish to scramble for military power. Only Russia, following the example of ancient Rome, promotes a scheme to enrich herself by relying upon military strength. Russia desires above all to enhance her military might on the strength of her increased national wealth. Indeed, Russia is the factory in which the evil of war in Europe is manufactured. But if this is the case, why doesn't Russia invade India at once? What Russia fears is not Great Britain so much as France, and not France so much as Prussia. Russia is afraid of a rear attack while she advances her forces toward the east. This is why the last time Prussia and France fought, Russia danced with joy and broke the Treaty of Crimea quickly by sending her fleet to the Black Sea.

"Thus, my guess is that once Prussian and French troops fight on the plains of Europe, Russian troops will immediately rush toward the east, kicking up sand. If this happens, the disaster of a Franco-Prussian war will not be limited to the European continent, and the Asian islands will be swept up into the conflict. Komun Island* will not be the only place seized by the British fleet and made into a base. In a nutshell, if Prussia and France compete in Europe, then Russia and Great Britain will vie for supremacy in Asia. This is the general situation of the world today.

"Ah, when Prussian and French troops fill the plains of Europe with the smell of gunpowder, and when British and Russian forces stir up the dust of combat on the Asian continent and create huge waves in Asian seas, can international law ever control the acts of violence which are called for by military strategies? And if international law should prove unreliable, by what means can a small nation protect itself?

"There is only one course to take: to abandon a sinking dinghy and leap aboard an unshakable ship as quickly as possible. This is the only safe policy—leave a precarious, small country and seize a safe, large country. But in a clear, shallow stream you cannot catch big fish; in ordinary times you cannot put such a daring strategem into practice. Right now, when ominous clouds are about to rise simultaneously from Europe and Asia, our small nation has a rare chance to turn a misfortune into a blessing. To turn the weak into the

---

* Komun Island is an island in the Strait of Korea which was briefly occupied by the British in 1885.

strong—such an opportunity comes only once in a th
years. Given these conditions, I am dumbfounded
easygoing attitude of our nation. Instead of moving immediately, like the thunder that booms out before one can
cover one's ears, we fidget and make a futile effort to preserve the country, relying on makeshift measures, like an
old peasant woman mending a rag."

At this point, Master Nankai took another drink and said,
"Let's summarize the Gentleman's ideas. The system of
democracy and equality is the purest and most perfect of
all systems, and all the nations of the world will surely
adopt it sooner or later. Since a small, weak nation can
never hope for a policy that ensures national wealth and
military strength, it should quickly adopt this perfect and
pure system. It should abolish its army and navy, abandon
its defenses that amount to less than a ten-thousandth of
those of the strong nations anyway, and stand on the basis
of intangible moral principles. By enthusiastically promoting learning, the small nation can make itself like a precisely sculpted work of art that strong nations will love, and
they will be unable to find it within themselves to violate
it.

'Mr. Champion's views should also be summarized.
European nations are concentrating on military competition. Once an explosion occurs, the disaster will likely
spread to Asia. Therefore, a small and weak nation should
take drastic measures: all the able-bodied men of the
country, battle armed, should conquer that large unnamed
country in order to open up vast new territory. Without
such a step, even if we tried to put our domestic affairs in
order, we would be forced to eliminate any lovers of nostalgia who would hinder the work of reform. Thus, the
plan to invade this foreign land must be implemented.

"Mr. Gentleman's ideas are pure and righteous; Mr.

Champion's ideas are uninhibited and extraordinary. Mr. Gentleman's ideas are strong liquor that makes me dizzy. They make my head swim. Mr. Champion's ideas are harsh poison that rends my stomach and rips my intestines. I am an old man. My deteriorating brain cannot possibly grasp or digest your ideas. Both of you should keep up with your efforts, and when the time comes, test your ideas in the real world. I'd be most content simply to observe."

The two guests also took another drink each and said to Master Nankai, "We have both emptied our hearts. Master, please criticize our ideas and instruct us. We ask this sincerely."

Master Nankai replied, "Mr. Gentleman's ideas derive from theoretical musings, both spoken and written, brewed in the minds of European scholars, but these opinions have not yet been practiced in the world. They are like dazzlingly attractive clouds. Mr. Champion's ideas, on the other hand, are what ancient leaders actually put into practice once in a hundred or a thousand years. Through them, these leaders achieved their fame. But such ideas are no longer practicable and they have become mere tricks of political jugglers. Dazzling clouds show great promise for the future, but they can only be enjoyed from afar. Political machinations are a rarely seen relic of the past, and they are amusing only when we meet them in history books. But clouds and machinations have no use in the here and now. Mr. Gentleman's ideas cannot be put into practice unless all the people of the nation cooperate, and Mr. Champion's ideas cannot be carried out unless the sovereign or the premier acts arbitrarily on his own authority. The ideas that both of you advocate are only empty words.

"Moreover, though Mr. Gentleman so vehemently insists that the god of evolution is powerful, the path of this god is crooked—it rises and falls, it turns to the left and to the right, it boards a boat or takes a carriage. It retreats while it seems to progress and moves forward while it seems to retreat. Contrary to what Mr. Gentleman has said, the path of this god is not a straight line, at least as defined by our geometry. If we mere mortals should presume to lead the god of evolution, inconceivable disaster would result. We have no choice but to follow the god on foot, with humility.

"In addition," the Master continued, "the law of evolution is so named because it is based on a careful observation of what has happened in the world. Therefore, the law of evolution accounts for the fact that human beings on earth fought among themselves at the very time of its creation.* Similarly, the law of evolution encompasses all stages of political progress: from monarchy through constitutionalism to democracy. Kings, presidents, aristocrats, and common people; boats with white sails and steam-powered warships; rifles and cannon; Buddhism, Confucianism, and Christianity—all the traces of human life and history are squarely within what scholars call the path of the god of evolution. In some European nations capital punishment has been abolished. This is a step forward in the progress of Europe. But some African tribes are cannibals, and this is itself a stage in the progress of African tribes. The god of evolution cannot be so easily pinned down. He possesses the greatest variety of affections, loves, preoccupations, and appetites.

"My dear Mr. Gentleman, you say that the god of evolution loves constitutionalism and democracy but hates despotism. Do you mean that in Turkey or in Persia there is no god of evolution? You say that the god of evolution loves the virtues of growth and nurture, but rejects the

* The *Book of Changes* (*Yi Jing*) expresses the theory that human society was primitive and chaotic at the time of the creation of the world.

123

violence of murder. Was the god of evolution absent when Xiang Yu buried alive the four hundred thousand soldiers of Zhao who surrendered themselves?*

"Who can presume to speak for the god of evolution? He preferred feudalism in the feudal period. He favors counties and prefectures now that there are counties and prefectures.† He favors national isolation in times of national isolation and trade in times of active commerce. He relishes boiled barley and rice as well as steak. He savors unrefined sakè as well as wine. He likes braided as well as tumbling hair. He loves the monochromatic water-colors of Chen Shitian as well as the oil paintings of Rembrandt.† Indeed, the god of evolution is the world's greatest lover of variety.

"But we should remember one thing that the god of evolution definitely hates. Politicians, especially, should remember it, for if politicians do not know what the god of evolution hates, unimaginable disaster will result. If we humble students speak and act without knowing what the god of evolution hates, we bring disaster only upon ourselves. If we write a book without knowing what the god of evolution hates, all that will happen is that the book will not sell. If we conspire against the government without knowing what the god hates, we will merely face impris-

---

* Xiang Yu (232–202 B.C.) was a general at the end of the Qin dynasty (221–206 B.C.). Although Xiang Yu did not execute Zhao soldiers, he is said to have buried alive some 200,000 soldiers who had surrendered to him. Professors Kuwabara and Shimada suggest that Chōmin's allusion might be to Bo Qi (c. 260 B.C.), another famous general of Qin (p. 247). At the battle of Changping, Bo Qi, after defeating the Zhao forces, massacred some 450,000 Zhao soldiers who had surrendered to him.
† In 1871 the Japanese government abolished the feudal domains (*han*) and divided the country into prefectures (*ken*) and counties (*gun*).
† Chen Shitian (1427–1509) was a painter of the Southern school of Chinese painting during the Ming dynasty (1368–1644).

onment or execution. But if a politician governs without knowing what the god of evolution hates, tens of millions of people will suffer. This is what we should fear.

"Just what is it that the god of evolution hates? Nothing other than talking and acting without regard to time and place. But no, that's not it exactly. Even if politicians administer a state without regard to time and place, and even if tens of millions of people consequently suffer, scholars who study the aftermath would surely say that there was a necessary cause for what happened. If the disaster resulted from a necessary cause, then it is by nature what the god of evolution loved and not what he hated. Thus, when asked to discuss the reform government of Wang Anshi the scholars will surely say: It happened because it had to happen.* In other words, everything that has happened from ancient times to date is what the god of evolution has loved. Then what exactly is it that the god of evolution hates? Simply this: trying to do what cannot be done at the given time and place. Mr. Gentleman, can what you have said possibly be done here and now? Or rather, is it something that can simply never be done?

"Mr. Gentleman, you have great respect for the god of evolution. Therefore, let me criticize what you've said according to your own standard according to the law of evolution. Please do not be offended.

"Mr. Gentleman, who advocates the system of equality, maintains that the institution of the aristocracy is what the god of evolution hates. He even compares titles to rocks blocking the god's path. But this is a grave error. If the god of evolution truly hated the five aristocratic titles, why would he keep supplementing the ranks of the aristocracy with new members? The Asian god of evolution, at least,

---

* Wang Anshi (1021–1086) was a social and political reformer of the Song dynasty.

125

loves the aristocracy. The old as well as the new aristocrats are all healthy and have hearty appetites.

"Imagine a midsummer epidemic of some horrible fever. Even though a solution of carbolic acid is poured onto the streets, the fever spreads until a hundred thousand corpses are piled up for cremation. But the aristocrats, old as well as new, are not at all affected by the disease and remain healthy. The poor—parents and children, husbands and wives—are sent to isolation wards in a long string of carriages. Another long string of carriages then carries them off to be cremated. But the aristocrats live in towering mansions, have their mistresses or maids fan them to provide cool breezes, and remain healthy, as if nothing abnormal were happening. In my opinion, the Asian god of evolution likes aristocrats and dislikes commoners. This is in direct opposition to what the Gentleman has said."

When he had said this, Master Nankai suddenly sat upright. "But what I have said is more or less a joke. Please forgive me, both of you."

Master Nankai took another drink. "Mr. Gentleman, you single-mindedly insist on democracy, but it seems that you have not yet completely grasped the essence of politics. What is it? Simply to let people, in so far as their will and intellect permit, enjoy the benefits of peace and happiness. If we choose a system which is not adapted to the will or the intellectual level of the people, how could they possibly obtain peace or happiness? Suppose democracy was established today in Turkey or Persia. The masses would be confused, start riots, and in the end cause civil war. The entire nation would be bathed in blood—it is inevitable.

"In addition, according to what Mr. Gentleman calls the law of evolution, the normal order of political progress is from despotism to constitutionalism, and from constitutionalism to democracy. To jump from despotism to de-

126

mocracy all at once is a violation of this order. Why? At a time when the concepts and images of kings, dukes, and marquises are deeply impressed upon the people's consciousness and, though invisible, act like an individual's protective deity or talisman, the people's minds would be utterly confused by the sudden introduction of democracy. This is a simple and precise psychological truth. In such a case, two or three individuals may rejoice, claiming that democracy is morally right, but what of the confusion and commotion of the masses? The logic of this is quite clear.

"Moreover, there are two kinds of rights that are commonly called people's rights. The people's rights of Great Britain and France are retrieved rights attained through the citizens' efforts. But there is another kind, in which people receive their rights as an imperial gift; these rights are bestowed as a favor from above. Because retrieved rights are obtained through the people's efforts, the number of rights can be determined by the will of the people. By contrast, bestowed rights are granted from above, so that the number of rights cannot be determined by the will of the people. Is it not an illogical leap to try to transform the people's bestowed rights, the moment they are granted, into retrieved rights?

I'm rather proud of the writing in this paragraph.

"It is true that civil wars are caused when the sovereign or the premier, relying on his power, does not restore the free rights in his keeping to the people. This prompted the people of Great Britain and France to take up the task of retrieving their rights. On the other hand, nothing is more beneficial for the government and the people, or for the ruler and his subjects, than for a sovereign or a premier to have a clear perception of the tendency of the times, to follow the will of the people, to try to suit their intellectual level, and graciously to bestow on them their free rights in proper amounts. It is better to sit still and make

127

do with ten *ryō* than to risk losing one's life to obtain a thousand *ryō*.* Further, the bestowed rights, no matter how limited, do not differ in substance from the retrieved rights. Therefore, if we preserve the rights given to us, treasure them, and nourish them with the marvelous influence of moral principles and the nutritive liquid called learning, our bestowed rights will gradually grow in range and substance as time progresses and history advances until they equal the retrieved rights of democratic nations. This is the true law of progress.

"I tell you, Mr. Gentleman, ideas are seeds planted in the field of the mind. If you truly love democracy, talk about it, write books about it, and sow its seeds in the minds of the people. Then, in several hundred years, democracy might flourish all over the country. Today, the plants of the sovereign and aristocrats are still rooted in the public mind. Isn't it wrong to try to gather a rich harvest of democracy immediately, simply because the seed of democracy has sprouted in your own brain?

"The public mind is a storehouse for the ideas of the past. All social undertakings are expressions of past ideas. Therefore, if we wish to build a new enterprise, we must first plant the necessary idea in the people's minds, so it, too, can someday become an established idea—an idea of the past. Why? An action always bears its fruit in the present, but an idea always has its roots in the past. Mr. Gentleman, please read your history. What has occurred in all nations is a result of the ideas of those nations. But ideas and actions do not align themselves in neat rows; they form a crooked line—and this line is the history of all nations.

"Ideas give birth to actions. Actions in turn give birth to new ideas. This endless flux is the essence of the path of the god of evolution. The god of evolution is not enshrined

* The *ryō* was an old monetary unit of gold or silver.

128

solemnly above the head of society, nor is he hiding under society's foot. Instead, he crouches in the public mind. He is an amalgamation of people's ideas. He forms a great circle of unity and completeness. Mr. Gentleman, you may worship an idea as it exists within your mind, but if you, a single individual, try to force the masses to worship it as an opinion of the god of evolution, it would be like placing a single dot with India ink on a piece of paper and trying to make the masses recognize the dot as a perfectly inscribed circle. This would be ideological despotism, and is precisely what the god of evolution does not like and what a scholar should be warned against.

"An age is silk or paper, ideas are colors, and great projects are paintings. A society of a given period is a painting that has already been completed. Mr. Gentleman, is it not madness to paint a picture of the future on a piece of paper called the present with pigments which are not yet completely ground? If you make diligent efforts now to refine your ideas or grind your pigments, a hundred years later the colors will pour richly onto the palette of society. At that point, if someone paints a picture on the piece of silk or paper of his present, the radiant colors you have mixed in his past will dazzle the eyes of all spectators, who will admire and praise the painting as a masterpiece surpassing those of Rubens or Poussin.

Not to be found either in the collected works of Victor Hugo or in the collected works of Lord Byron.

Beautifully put

"Further, you both insist on maintaining views that are poles apart, one trying to move forward, blindly groping toward new ideas which are not yet born, and the other trying to move backward, blindly admiring an old-fashioned play that was performed long ago. Your main ideas may seem as incompatible as ice and hot coals, but I think that you share a common disease: excessive anxiety. You have both seen the powerful nations of Europe maintaining a

129

million strong soldiers, building ten million battleships, biting and grappling with each other, and coming frequently to wreak havoc on Asia. You have thus become overly concerned that these powerful Europeans will surely invade us someday, equipped with a hundred or a thousand battleships. This explains why you hold such extreme views.

"Mr. Gentleman wishes to adopt democracy, abolish the military forces that signify hostility, and avoid attack by gaining moral superiority over Europe. Mr. Champion wishes to send off a great force, conquer another country, expand territories, and gain great profits by capitalizing on the squabbles in Europe. Both of you are worrying too much about the situation of European nations.

"As I see it, even though the situation may seem critical because Prussia and France are now vigorously expanding their armaments, it is not so. If their expansion of armaments were on a small scale, an explosion might indeed occur, but since they're building up their armed forces on a large scale, no explosion is possible. Why not? Haven't the two of you seen a child making a snowball in winter? At first, when the snowball is not very big, the child can easily roll it back and forth or right and left. But when the snowball becomes huge, the child can no longer push it, no matter how hard he may try. Two children—Prussia and France—are competing with each other in their endless efforts to see who can make the bigger snowball. If Prussia increases its troops by ten thousand, France also adds ten thousand; if Prussia adds twenty thousand, so does France. Thus, the snowball grows larger every year. In the meantime, Russia and Great Britain look on, waiting for the two snowballs to collide. But as long as snow remains in his own yard, each child concentrates on making his snowball larger, until he cannot easily push it outside his gate. By the time all the snow is gone in the yard, the two snowballs will have broken to pieces.

130

"Further, even though the idea of world peace may not yet be realized, it is the natural course of events that in international society, the influence of moral principles will gradually expand while physical force will gradually diminish. This is the true course of what Mr. Gentleman calls the god of evolution. Therefore, even though Russia desires to expand into Asia, seize what territories it can, and attack Great Britain's India, she has not yet done so. On the surface, it only seems as if every nation in its foreign policy values physical force and slights moral principles. In reality, however, the situation is not as extreme as most people imagine. If one of the great powers—Prussia, France, Great Britain, or Russia—were especially strong and far surpassed the other three, it might act violently at will, relying on its physical strength and disregarding international law completely. But this is not the case. The balance of power of all four nations is roughly maintained, so they must observe international law, more or less. This is why many small nations have been spared the disaster of annexation by stronger nations.

"In addition, a state is a mixture of many desires. Consisting of the sovereign, the government officials, parliament, and the common people, it has a highly complex structure. Therefore, a state cannot decide its direction or start a movement as freely as an individual can. If it could, strong nations would always tyrannize others without restraint, and weak nations would always have to suffer the disastrous consequences. Fortunately, such is not the case. If a nation wishes to mobilize ten thousand soldiers and send a hundred battleships, first the sovereign examines the plan, then the premier, and then the officials. Then the parliament and the newspapers argue its merits. Clearly, a state is not like an individual, who can pull up the hem of his garment, grab a club, and set out on foot to fight. This is how General Gordon lost his life in the desert of Arabia.

131

Admiral Courbet died suffering from the heat of Annam for the same reason. Thus, the soldiers of Europe are like a tiger or a lion, and their parliaments and newspapers serve as cages.

"Moreover, international law and the balance of power both provide invisible restraints on the animal's limbs. That fierce lion or tiger cannot bite at will, although it may gape horribly. Therefore I affirm that Mr. Gentleman's democracy and Mr. Champion's plan of invasion are both the results of excessive worry over the powerful nations of Europe."

At this point the two guests said in unison, "But Master, if they're audacious enough to attack us some day, how would you deal with them?"

Master Nankai said, "If they do not fear the criticism of other nations, do not respect the obligations of international law, disregard the arguments of their own parliaments, and dare to attack us with treacherous hearts, we must simply resist with all our strength. We would all become soldiers, defending ourselves at strategic points or attacking the invaders by surprise. We would advance or retreat, appear or disappear, and aim for unpredictability and the element of surprise. We would also kindle the passion of our officers and soldiers by emphasizing that the enemies are the 'intruders' and we are the 'masters' and that the enemies are immoral and we are moral. If we did these things, who can say that we could not defend ourselves? Our military people would naturally devise excellent strategies to deal with the invasion.

"If our Asian soldiers are ultimately no match for European soldiers, it is inevitable that Mr. Gentleman's democratic nation and Mr. Champion's new and enlarged nation would both fall. I certainly don't have any great master plan. But I'm not alone. Great Britain, France, and the others attack one another or defend themselves, but they don't have a master plan either. In short, although our Asian troops are not sufficient as invading forces, they are indeed sufficient as defense forces. Therefore, if we educate our soldiers well, make them practice regularly, and keep their morale high in times of peace, why should we worry that we cannot defend ourselves in times of war? Why should we follow Mr. Gentleman and wait to be killed without attempting any resistance? Or why should we incur our neighbor's hostility by following Mr. Champion's plan?

"Of course, I have no idea which country Mr. Champion refers to as a certain large nation of Africa or Asia. But if that nation is in Asia, we should ally ourselves to it, and become brother nations sworn to help each other in an emergency. Thereby we can save ourselves from danger. It is indeed a poor policy to take up arms blindly, to provoke our neighbors and make enemies thoughtlessly, and to cause innocent citizens to die from bullet wounds.

"Take China as an example. Because of its customs, manners, culture, national character, and geography, we as a small Asian nation should always maintain a strong, friendly relationship with China and try not to cause hostilities. If we step up our nation's production, then China, with its vast territory and large population, would become our chief market and a wellspring of inexhaustible profit. Even without taking this point into consideration, to be temporarily obsessed with the idea of exalting national prestige or to instigate a blind quarrel under the pretext of trivial linguistic misunderstandings is, in my opinion, most irrational.

"Some may argue that China has long been trying to take revenge on Japan. Even if we try to show every courtesy, deepen our friendship, and maintain a good relationship,

133

China, because of its relations with a certain other small nation, always harbors anger against us.* Thus we cannot rule out the possibility that if given the chance China might form an alliance with strong European nations to exclude our country and make us a prey of strong nations for its own profit. But in my view, China's thinking has not gone that far. In many cases, one nation's hostility toward another is caused not by real situations but by false rumors. If one examines the real situation, there is no need for suspicion. But if one's conjectures are based solely upon rumor, the situation may look extremely grave. A nation's suspicion toward others is its neurosis. If you wear blue glasses, everything you see will look blue. I always find it a pity that the glasses of diplomats are not transparent and colorless.

"Thus, two countries go to war not because they love war but because they fear it. We fear our enemy and hurry to put our military forces in order. Then our enemy fears us and hurries to put his military forces in order. The paranoia of both sides intensifies as days and months go by. We also have the newspapers, which report real situations and false rumors side by side, indiscriminately. In extreme cases, a newspaper reporter writes a 'paranoid' article, colors it in an unusual way, and spreads it throughout the world. The nerves of the two nations which fear each other then become more and more distracted. Their governments begin to say, 'Take the initiative, and we will win. Why

* The "linguistic misunderstandings" Master cites may refer to the Treaty of Kanghwa, which was forced on Korea by Japan in 1876 and defined Korea as an independent state. China interpreted the treaty as an affirmation that Korea was a vassal state subject to Chinese intervention if China deemed it necessary, thus contradicting the definition of Korea as an independent state. Professor Oh states that the treaty "gave rise to an intense rivalry between China and Japan over Korea." See Bonnie B. Oh, "Sino-Japanese Rivalry in Korea, 1876–1885," in *The Chinese and the Japanese: Essays in Political and Cultural Interactions*, ed. Akira Iriye (Princeton, New Jersey: Princeton University Press, 1980), p. 37.

don't we initiate the attack?' The fear these two nations share rapidly reaches its peak and leads of its own accord to war. In the past as well as today, this is how wars actually start in every nation. If one of the two nations is not suffering from paranoia, war will not usually break out. And even if war does begin, the sane nation will adopt defense as its main strategy. It will keep its presence of mind, and can thus claim that truth and justice are on its side. Thereby it will not be judged harshly by history.

"On the other hand, some may argue that China has a truly vast territory, but that the country has degenerated and now faces revolution. Unless a hero emerges from the masses and seizes the power of the sovereign, China's collapse cannot be prevented. But this view is a simplistic conjecture derived from the length of each reign from ancient China to the current ruling Aisingioro family.* It does not fit the present situation. Why not? When compared with how long the old dynasties lasted before they fell, the reign of the Aisingioro family must be considered ancient, decrepit, and destined to collapse. But, fortunately, because the invigorating breeze of European civilization has come blowing from the west, the old tree that was about to die has suddenly regained its vitality. Its branches and leaves have become green and its shadow is spreading in four directions once again.

"In addition, the government administrators in the imperial court, who play vital roles in current Chinese society, are all intelligent and talented. They are paying special attention to building up the army and navy, and are buying the fruits of European civilization with China's rich financial resources. More battleships are built day by day; more fortresses are being built month by month; the

* Aisingioro was the name of the last ruling family of the Qing dynasty, which ended in 1911.

135

military structure is being completely changed to imitate the European model. How can such a nation be disdained as an opponent? Clearly a sound diplomatic policy is based on maintaining peaceful and friendly relations with every nation of the world, adopting a defensive strategy when it is absolutely necessary, avoiding the hardship and expense of sending troops far away, and trying to lighten the burden on the shoulders of the people. Unless we reveal symptoms of diplomatic paranoia, why should China consider us an enemy?''

Master Nankai prevaricates.

The Gentleman then spoke up. "Master's argument, filled with metaphors and epithets, is most delightful, but what is the main point? I cannot help feeling as if I were trying to catch a shadow. Master, please give us the main point of your discourse."

The Champion joined in. "Master's argument does not incorporate anything that we have said. Please instruct us by giving your views on a great plan for our nation's future."

Master Nankai said, "I would simply establish constitutionalism, reinforce the dignity and glory of the emperor above and increase the happiness and peace of all the people below. I would establish Upper and Lower houses of Parliament. Aristocrats would he assigned to the Upper House and membership would be hereditary. Members of the Lower House would be chosen by election. That's all. As for detailed statutes, we should examine the existing constitutions of Europe and America and adopt what should be adopted. Such matters as these cannot be treated fully in a brief discussion.

"In framing diplomatic policy, peace and friendship should be the basic rule. Unless our national pride is damaged, we should not act in a high-handed manner or take up arms. Restrictions on speech, publication, and other activities should be gradually eased, and education, commerce, and industry should be gradually promoted. Or something like that.''

Upon hearing these words, the two guests laughed and said, "We've heard that Master's ideas are unusual. But if they are what you've just said, they're not at all unusual. Nowadays, even children and servants are familiar with them."

Master Nankai sat up straight and said, "On a topic meant for casual conversation, there is no harm in competing for novelty or strangeness, or in making a joke for temporary amusement. But in discussing such a topic as the master plan for our country's next hundred years, how could we amuse ourselves by consciously seeking the bizarre or by stressing novelty for its own sake? Still, since I am stubborn, negligent, and ignorant of the trends of the times, I'm afraid my speech has often been irrelevant. It probably hasn't matched your expectations.''

The three men exchanged cups once again. The European brandy was already gone and they sent for some bottles of beer. They continued to quench their thirst and went on talking cordially for a while, when suddenly a rooster next door announced the dawn. Taken by surprise, the two guests said, "We must be going now.''

Master Nankai laughed and said, "You didn't notice, did you? That rooster has crowed twice already since you arrived. When you return home, you'll realize that two or three years have gone by. Such is the calendar of my house.'' The two guests also broke into laughter and finally took their leave. About ten days later Master Nankai completed this book.

The two guests never returned. According to rumor, the Gentleman of Western Learning went to North America and the Champion went to Shanghai. Master Nankai, as always, keeps on drinking.

The "weathermark" identifies this book as a production of Weatherhill, publishers of fine books on Asia and the Pacific. Supervising editor: Jeffrey Hunter. Book design and typography: Miriam F. Yamaguchi.